Ice Cream & Frozen Desserts

LONNIE GANDARA
Writer

ELAINE RATNER
Editor

VICTOR BUDNIK
Photographer

KAREN HAZARIAN
KATHLEEN VOLKMANN
Food Stylists

AMY GLENN
Photographic Stylist

CALIFORNIA CULINARY ACADEMY

Lonnie Gandara is a teacher, lecturer, cook, culinary event organizer, caterer, food consultant, author, and Merchandise Director for California Public Markets. She is the author of the California Culinary Academy book *Fish & Shellfish*. She holds an advanced certificate from Le Cordon Bleu in Paris, France, and has studied cooking in Italy, Mexico, Hong Kong, Bangkok, and Singapore. She is a member of the International Association of Cooking Professionals, the American Institute of Wine and Food, and the San Francisco Professional Food Society.

The California Culinary Academy In the forefront of American institutions leading the culinary renaissance in this country, the California Culinary Academy in San Francisco has gained a reputation as one of the most outstanding professional chef training schools in the world. With a teaching staff recruited from the best restaurants of Western Europe, the Academy educates students from around the world in the preparation of classical cuisine. The recipes in this book were created in consultation with the chefs of the Academy. For information about the Academy, write the Office of the Dean, California Culinary Academy, 625 Polk Street, San Francisco, CA 94102.

Front Cover
As any ice cream lover knows, the best ice creams are the ones you make at home. Combine them with your own freshly made toppings (see pages 25–33) for the kind of sundaes, sodas, and banana splits your favorite soda fountain used to make. For more soda fountain treats, see pages 34–43.

Title Page
The ice cream scoop has come a long way, from the first mechanical scoops that looked like oversized candle snuffers to today's sleek models with antifreeze in their hollow handles.

Back Cover
Upper Left: Frozen pops made from yogurt, pudding, or fruit (see page 59) are a quick-and-easy after-school treat.

Upper Right: Frozen Mango Mousse served in a delicate Coconut Tulip (see page 67) is an elegant springtime dessert.

Lower Left: Mile-High Strawberry Pie (see page 115) is light and refreshing, with afternoon tea or anytime.

Lower Right: You'll quickly build a repertoire of homemade ice creams and sauces, then it's a snap to create your own distinctive parfaits and coupes (see page 42).

Special Thanks to
Beaver Bros. Antiques, Biordi Art Imports, Virginia Breier, Claire's Antique Linens and Gifts, Linda Hersh Collings, Craig Colton, Cookbook Village, Jim Dodge, Peggy Fallon, Fillamento, Bea and Marty Glenn, Nancy Glenn and Ward Finer, Judy Goldsmith, Leonard D. Grotta, Hard Rock Cafe, Jay Harlow, Shawn Harris, Michael Heller, Kass Kaspiac, La Parisienne, Laura Ashley Inc., Dianne McKenzie, Mel's drive-in, Roman Marble, Tina Salter, Roldan Tavio-Reyes, The Alsatian Kitchen, The Attic, The Campbells, The Daily Scoop, The Producer, Tiffany & Co., Upstairs Downstairs, Bill Volkmann, Mrs. Daniel G. Volkmann, Wedgwood, Williams-Sonoma, Xanadu Gallery/Folk Art International.

Contributors

Calligraphers
Keith Carlson, Chuck Wertman

Additional Photographers
Laurie Black, Academy photography, pages 66, 106; Alan Copeland, Academy photography, pages 39, 83, 87, 105; Russ Fischella, author, at left; Kit Morris, chefs, at left; Richard Tauber, pages 14, 16, 24, 35, 50, 51, 57, 67, 82

Additional Food Stylist
Clay Wollard, pages 14, 16, 24, 35, 50, 51, 57, 67, 82

Photographer's Assistants
Denise Cannon, Caroline Cory

Copy Chief
Melinda E. Levine

Copyeditors
Andrea Connolly, Judy Ziajka

Indexer
Elinor Lindheimer

Proofreader
Judith Dunham

Editorial Assistants
Tamara Mallory, Raymond Quinton

Composition by
Linda M. Bouchard, Bob Miller

Series Format Designed by
Linda Hinrichs, Carol Kramer

Production by
Lezlly Freier

Color Separations by
Color Tech. Corp.

Lithographed in the U.S.A. by
Webcrafters, Inc.

The California Culinary Academy series is produced by the staff of Ortho Information Services.

Publisher
Robert J. Dolezal

Editorial Director
Christine Robertson

Production Director
Ernie S. Tasaki

Series Managing Editor
Sally W. Smith

Systems Manager
Katherine L. Parker

Address all inquiries to
Ortho Information Services
P.O. Box 5047
San Ramon, CA 94583

Chevron Chemical Company
6001 Bollinger Canyon Road
San Ramon, CA 94583

C O N T E N T S

Ice Cream & Frozen Desserts

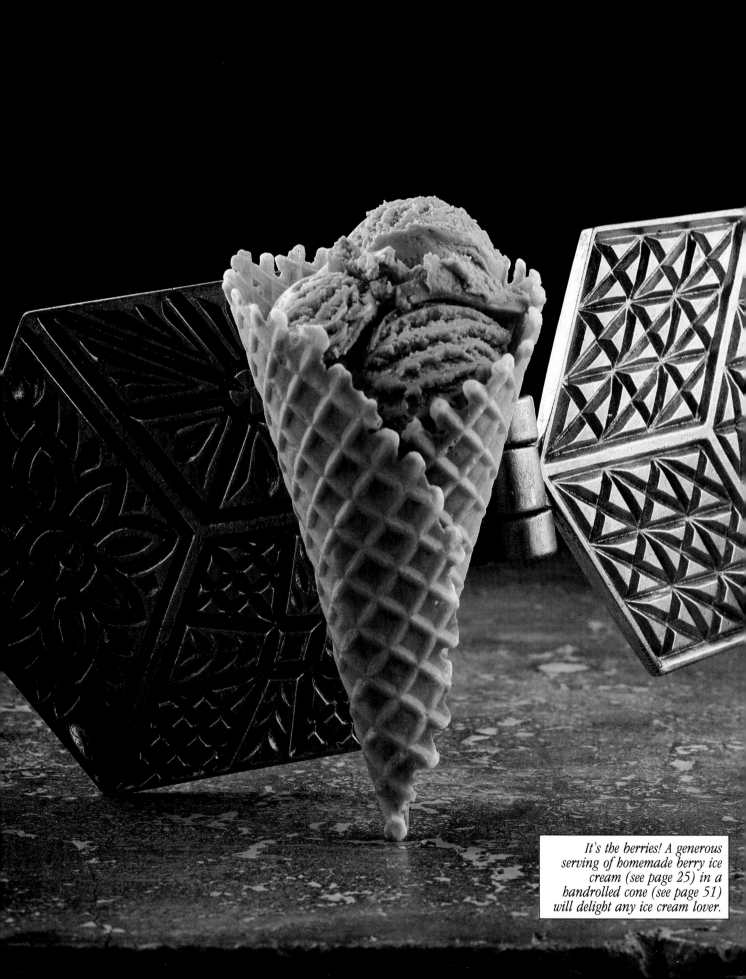

*It's the berries! A generous
serving of homemade berry ice
cream (see page 25) in a
handrolled cone (see page 51)
will delight any ice cream lover.*

Making Ice Cream at Home

Iscream, you scream, we all scream for ice cream. As children we delighted in ice cream cones and sandwiches, sundaes and banana splits. As adults we still do. Ice cream is a universal treat; travel just about anywhere, and you can enjoy it with the natives. Birthday parties and afternoons at the beach absolutely demand it. Dinner party guests adore it. Whether it's shaped into an elaborate bombe, set aflame with brandy, topped with sauce, or just scooped into a cone, ice cream is a tasty, refreshing, happy dessert. With so many inexpensive, simple-to-operate, mess-free ice cream machines now on the market, any home kitchen can be a first-class ice cream parlor, every dessert-loving cook an ice cream pro.

WHO INVENTED ICE CREAM?

A popular legend attributes the invention of ice cream to the Roman emperor Nero, who in the first century A.D. sent runners to fetch snow from the top of nearby mountains and then had it flavored with wine and fruit juices. In truth, historical records suggest that ice cream originated much earlier. There is evidence that the ancient Chinese were already making water ices at the beginning of recorded history, and they were probably doing so well before. From China frozen desserts spread to Arabia, India, and Persia.

Marco Polo encountered flavored ices on his journeys to the East and was responsible for introducing them to Italy. The dessert he introduced was probably the forerunner of what we would call a milk ice (rather than a water ice, or sherbet), goat's milk probably having been added to the original Chinese water ices by the Arabians. The art of making frozen desserts in Italy was refined with the discovery of salt as an aid to freezing. Ice cream (along with another Italian innovation, the dinner fork) was introduced to France in the sixteenth century by Catherine de Médicis. From there it quickly spread to England and then to the rest of Europe.

The dessert we now know as ice cream—at first called cream ice—was introduced by a French chef to King Charles I of England early in the seventeenth century. Initially it was available only to royalty and court nobility, but by the end of the seventeenth century, commoners too were indulging in frozen desserts. By 1676 there were 250 shops selling ice cream and ices in Paris alone, and the French government gave ice cream vendors official status as a trade guild.

Despite the rapid spread of ices and ice cream throughout Europe, the enormous and widespread popularity that ice cream enjoys today is a relatively modern, and largely American, phenomenon, attributable in no small way to the development of reliable refrigeration in the twentieth century. The familiar hand-cranked ice cream churn was invented in 1846 by an American woman named Nancy Johnson (about whom little else is known). The first ice cream cone evidently was sold at the St. Louis World Exposition of 1904, when an ice cream vendor ran out of dishes and started substituting rolled-up wafers from a neighboring concessionaire. During the 1920s a variety of frozen desserts were invented in rapid succession, including the Eskimo pie, the Good Humor bar, and the Popsicle. In 1939 a machine for making soft ice cream, by incorporating a great deal of air into the mixture, was perfected, and fast-food businesses serving ice cream or ice milk quickly proliferated. Unfortunately, as the manufacture of ice cream became big business in the United States, quality often suffered. Gelatin and milk were introduced into sherbets; flour and whole eggs were added to ice cream, and the amount of fresh cream was drastically reduced.

Today ice cream and frozen desserts continue to gain in popularity, and many commercial manufacturers are returning to stricter quality standards. A new generation of home ice cream freezers—smaller, easier to use, and more efficient than earlier versions—are inspiring ice cream enthusiasts to make homemade frozen desserts on a regular basis, not just for the occasional special party. Across America thousands of electric ice cream machines and prechilled canisters now stand ready to swing into action at a moment's notice.

ICE CREAM FREEZERS

An ice cream churn or freezer is really the only specialized piece of equipment needed for making ice cream at home. There are four basic types to choose from.

SALT-AND-ICE BUCKET FREEZER

The bucket freezer is the traditional ice cream churn that most of us remember from childhood. It has a large bucket with a smaller canister fitted into it. Traditionally the bucket was made of wood and needed to be soaked in water before using to prevent leaks. Today most machines come with a plastic or fiberglass bucket. The canister, made of stainless steel, has a removable lid. Inside is a stationary paddle called a dasher. Its blades are usually wood, plastic, or another soft substance and are positioned so that they gently scrape the inside of the canister as it turns. The canister is continuously rotated by either a hand crank or an electric motor, while a mixture of about three fourths crushed ice and one fourth rock salt in the bucket freezes the ice cream inside the canister. For convenience, some models work with ice cubes and ordinary table salt.

Bucket freezers usually cost $25 to $50. Hand-cranked models are less expensive but require 20 to 30 minutes of cranking for each batch of ice cream. Units equipped with electric motors produce slightly better results because of their consistent speed. Both models make excellent ice cream, but they do require ice and salt. Be aware that some bucket freezers won't hold whole ice cubes, so the ice must be crushed before it is added to the machine.

The texture of the finished ice cream depends on how fast it is processed. The slower the freezing

Today's home chef has a wide selection of ice cream makers to choose from, ranging from the old-fashioned crank-type to the new prechilled canister.

process, the smoother the texture. You can control the rate of freezing by varying the amount of salt you use with the ice. Use about three quarters of a standard 26-ounce box of salt for relatively fast freezing and excellent across-the-board results. Using a whole box of salt shortens the freezing time, producing an icier texture; using half a box lengthens the freezing time and gives a finer, smoother texture.

REFRIGERATOR-FREEZER UNIT

Some ice cream freezers are designed to fit inside the freezing compartment of a refrigerator, with the power cord snaking out through the closed door. An electric motor churns the ice cream and drives a small fan that circulates the cold air around the canister. The canister is stationary; the dasher turns. This type of freezer costs between $25 and $50—if you can find one. Its major advantage is that it doesn't require salt and ice.

PRECHILLED CANISTER FREEZER

The prechilled canister freezer is the newest type of ice cream machine. It is sometimes called a Donvier-type freezer after the Japanese company that invented it. It features a sealed, hollow metal canister that is filled with a special coolant. The canister must be frozen in the freezer compartment of a refrigerator for 24 to 48 hours before it is used. Then the canister is filled with chilled ice cream mixture, and a lid with a crank-and-dasher assembly is placed over it. The crank is rotated by hand every 2 or 3 minutes until the mixture freezes, which usually takes 12 to 18 minutes. Canister freezers generally cost $30 to $50, depending on size (the largest available so far is 1 quart). The major disadvantage of this type of machine is that the canister takes considerable space in the freezing compartment. The primary advantages are that it's easy to

use and it yields a surprisingly good texture—if the ice cream is eaten immediately. Because little air is incorporated during the churning process, the ice cream from this machine becomes very hard when stored.

FREEZER WITH SELF-CONTAINED REFRIGERATION

The self-contained freezer is the Rolls-Royce of ice cream machines. Freezing coils are wrapped around the canister, and a motorized dasher mixes the ice cream as it freezes. It is the easiest machine to use: Just pour in the ice cream mixture and turn on the freezer. Because of the constant beating of the dasher, this type of machine makes ice cream with a very smooth texture. Its chief drawbacks are its high price—$400 to $600—and the amount of counter space it occupies. It isn't a good idea to store self-contained machines away from where they are used; if moved, most must be left stationary for 24 hours before being used to allow the refrigerant to settle.

OTHER ICE CREAM–MAKING EQUIPMENT

Preparing ice cream to be frozen doesn't require much equipment. The bowls, spoons, and saucepans you use for everyday cooking will fill most of your needs. The items listed here are helpful but not mandatory for making ice cream and other frozen desserts.

Blender or Food Processor Either a food processor or blender may be used to purée fruit for ice creams and sherbets.

Candy Thermometer Using a candy thermometer is the best way to keep track of the changes sugar goes through as it is heated (see page 16). The small instant-read thermometers sold in cookware and hardware stores also serve this purpose, in addition to being useful for baking and roasting. Be sure to get one that measures up to 260° F.

Ice Cream Spades and Scoops

Spades and scoops are usually made from a solid casting of sturdy aluminum to eliminate the possibility of bent handles. Nonstick scoops contain a fluid antifreeze to ensure easy release of the ice cream. It is helpful to dip scoops without coolant into warm water between servings. Mechanical ice cream scoops have an arc-shaped blade that sweeps across the interior of the bowl to release the ice cream. The numbers imprinted on the handles of many scoops indicate how many scoops of that size can be removed from 1 quart of ice cream. Mechanical stainless steel scoops come in a variety of bowl shapes and sizes, ranging from a tiny, 1-inch sphere (number 100) to a 2½-inch-long oval (number 30). Ice cream scoops are also useful for serving individual portions of other foods, such as rice or potatoes.

Madeleine Pans These French pans are for baking the delicate little cakes made famous by novelist Marcel Proust. Each pan has 12 scallop-shaped indentations that each hold about ¾ ounce of batter.

Miniature Muffin Tins Miniature muffin tins, often sold as gem-sized pans, are useful in baking as well as for making bite-sized confections. The interior of each muffin cup is 1½ or 2 inches in diameter and holds ¾ to 1 fluid ounce.

Mixer A handheld or countertop mixer is useful for combining egg yolks and sugar, beating egg whites, and blending other commonly used ingredients. Although considerably more expensive, freestanding countertop mixers are usually more efficient and of better quality, and they free your hands to complete other chores while the machine does the mixing.

Molds Plastic or stainless steel molds are useful for forming ice cream into special shapes and for making frozen desserts with more than one flavor of ice cream. Although some molds are made specifically for frozen desserts, any type of mold of an appropriate size will work. To unmold a frozen dessert, gently immerse the mold nearly to the top in warm water to soften the ice cream around the edges. Then place a plate or serving tray upside down over the mold and invert.

Plastic molds for making frozen pops for children are available in many variety stores. A set consists of six molds, each capable of holding about ¼ cup liquid, fit into a tray that keeps them upright during freezing. These sets are often equipped with their own reusable plastic sticks. Wooden ice cream sticks inserted into 4-ounce paper drinking cups make acceptable substitutes, although you must wait until the pops are partially frozen before positioning the sticks.

Parchment Rolls of parchment paper can often be found in the section of the grocery store where you find waxed paper, foil, and plastic wrap. Parchment is invaluable for lining baking pans because the paper easily peels off the finished dessert. Waxed paper can be used as a substitute, as can an ordinary brown paper bag. Avoid using recycled paper, however, as it may contain harmful chemicals.

Pizzelle Iron *Pizzelles* are thin, decoratively patterned Italian wafer cookies, baked in a special iron similar to a waffle iron. They can be left flat or formed into cups, cylinders, or ice cream cones (see page 51). A manual pizzelle iron is heated directly on a stovetop burner. Electric pizzelle irons are thermostatically controlled to produce even heat. It is much easier to obtain satisfactory results with an electric iron.

Stainless Steel Mixing Bowls Large stainless steel bowls with flat bottoms are best for making ice cream. Most double boilers are too small for the quantities involved in making ice cream; a stainless steel

Fortunately, most of the equipment useful for making ice cream, such as bowls, spoons, a whisk, and a mixer, is normally found in the well stocked kitchen.

9

*The way you present ice
cream and other frozen
desserts can be as simple
or elaborate as you choose.
A selection of molds and
scoops adds variety to
your presentation and
gives it professional flair.*

bowl placed over a large kettle of
boiling water is an excellent substitute. Stainless steel is better than glass
or ceramic because it can be trans-
ferred from the heat to an ice-water
bath without any danger of breaking.
Unlike other metals, stainless steel
does not react with common ice
cream ingredients, such as acidic
fruits; aluminum and copper tend to
discolor when they come in contact
with acids and can give ice cream a
metallic taste.

**Stainless Steel or Wooden
Spoons** Stainless steel or wooden
spoons are preferred for ice cream-
making because they do not react
with acidic ingredients and can toler-
ate extreme temperature changes.

Storage Containers Ice cream
should always be stored in a covered,
airtight container, so that it doesn't
absorb odors from other foods, and
free moisture doesn't form ice crystals
on its surface. Any plastic container
with a tight-fitting lid is fine. If the
container is less than half full, press
a sheet of plastic wrap on the surface
of the ice cream to keep air out.

Wire Whisk In addition to perform-
ing mixing tasks when an electric
mixer isn't available, a whisk is
handy for stirring custard mixtures
on the stove.

Wooden Ice Cream Sticks The
flat, 5-inch-long wooden sticks used
for commercial ice cream bars can
be purchased at stores that specialize
in candy-making or party supplies
and occasionally can even be found
in grocery stores.

Zester A zester is a simple tool con-
sisting of a ¾-inch-long stainless
steel strip with tiny round blades
(similar to those on a grater) attached to a plastic handle. When the
tool is drawn with gentle pressure
across the skin of any citrus fruit, the
fragrant and flavorful "zest" is removed in very thin strips, leaving the
bitter pith behind.

ICE CREAM

Ice cream is a smooth, rich, frozen dessert made from egg yolks, milk, cream, sugar, and flavorings. Universal in its appeal, it is common in the cuisines of almost all countries. In France it is called *glace*, in Italy *gelato*. There are two general types of ice cream: cooked custard-based and uncooked Philadelphia-style.

BASIC INGREDIENTS

For ice cream to have a smooth, creamy texture, both the water molecules and the fat globules in the mixture must be suspended evenly, so that the ice crystals that form during freezing are very small. The basic ice cream ingredients, in addition to contributing flavor, help that to happen.

Many commercial ice cream manufacturers use emulsifiers and stabilizers to improve the texture of their products, to mask or compensate for inferior ingredients, or to achieve an extended shelf life. Such artificial ingredients are never needed in ice cream made in small quantities at home with fresh, wholesome ingredients. There are also homemade ice cream recipes that call for such ingredients as cornstarch, instant vanilla pudding, gelatin, and flour in an attempt to simulate the texture produced by more expensive ingredients. Anyone who has tasted good homemade ice cream, made with pure, high-quality ingredients, will find it hard to offer such pseudo-flavors to family and guests.

Cream The butterfat in cream is primarily responsible for providing the rich, smooth texture of ice cream. In general, the higher the proportion of butterfat, the richer and smoother the ice cream. However, resist the temptation to substitute whipping cream for the half-and-half or milk in an ice cream recipe. Too much cream greatly increases the chance of producing ice cream flecked with butter. As a general rule, do not exceed a ratio of 75 percent cream to 25 percent milk.

Tips

... ON PRECOOLING

It is important to cool an ice cream mixture thoroughly before churning it. It may be cooled slowly in the refrigerator or rapidly over an ice-water bath. If the mixture is warmer than 40° F when the freezing process begins, the increased churning time it will require is likely to produce flecks of butter, especially in those recipes that call for a high proportion of cream to milk. Although harmless, butter flecks are unpleasant and will ruin the fine texture of homemade ice cream. (Should butter form in a batch of ice cream, allow the ice cream to melt in the refrigerator. When the mixture is liquid, strain it through a fine sieve to remove the butter, then refreeze. The resulting ice cream will not be as smooth as if the recipe had been prepared properly, but it will be tasty and free of butter.)

... ON EXPANSION DURING FREEZING

When filling an ice cream machine with ice cream mixture, stop at least 2 inches below the top of the canister. As ice cream freezes, it expands slightly. More important, the churning action incorporates air. This aeration, called loft or overrun, improves the texture of the finished ice cream and helps prevent it from becoming a solid block of ice. If the freezing canister is filled two thirds full and the finished ice cream reaches the top, the overrun is approximately 50 percent; if the canister is filled three quarters full and the ice cream reaches the top, the over-run is approximately 30 percent. U.S. government (FDA) standards allow for as much as 100 percent overrun in commercial ice cream (meaning that the final product is 50 percent air). High-quality ice cream has 20 percent to 50 percent overrun. By specifying that commercial ice cream must weigh at least 4½ pounds per gallon, the government ensures that overrun does not exceed 100 percent. Most homemade ice creams and premium commercial ice creams weigh close to twice that much.

... ON STORING AND SERVING TEMPERATURES

Ice cream and other frozen desserts should be stored at low temperatures to prolong their shelf life and protect their texture and flavor. Between 0° and 10° F (-18° to -23° C) is ideal. Ice cream should be allowed to warm slightly before serving; about 30° F is an ideal serving temperature. If a container of ice cream is firmly frozen, transfer it from the freezer to the refrigerator 20 to 30 minutes before serving or leave it at room temperature for 10 to 15 minutes. Be careful not to let ice cream thaw too much; repeated thawing and refreezing will destroy its texture.

... ON RIPENING

Ice cream custard bases can be made in advance (up to 48 hours before the ice cream is to be frozen) and left to "ripen" in the freezer for several hours before serving. This improves the texture and allows time for the flavors to intermingle. Most homemade ice creams should be kept frozen for no more than a day or two. Ice cream stored for long periods develops ice crystals on top and takes on a heavy, undesirable texture. Fortunately, homemade ice cream is so delicious few cooks ever encounter this problem.

Using the freshest, purest ingredients makes all the difference. Friends and family will appreciate the rich, intense flavors of homemade ice cream free of any preservatives or additives.

Eggs Egg yolks are cooked to form the custard base used in many ice cream recipes. They act as emulsifiers; that is, they keep the fat globules in milk and cream from clumping together. Use large eggs for all the recipes in this book. Yolks are most easily separated from whites when eggs are cold, but egg whites at room temperature provide more volume when whisked. Egg whites may be frozen until needed, then thawed in the refrigerator.

Fruit Most fruits used to flavor ice cream contain naturally occurring pectin and a certain amount of fiber. Both of these substances help to keep milk fat and water molecules in an even suspension as they freeze.

Milk Milk fat forms small globules in the ice cream mixture that help to keep the water molecules dispersed. The emulsifying action of cooked egg yolks helps keep these small fat globules from clumping together as they are churned. If they do form clumps, they will produce butter.

Sugar Water in which sugar has been dissolved has a freezing point below 32° F. Because of the sugar present, not all the water in ice cream freezes. Sugar thus helps keep ice cream from becoming a solid block of ice.

CUSTARD-BASED ICE CREAM

Traditional, rich, custard-based ice cream is sometimes referred to as French custard. Egg yolks are cooked with sugar, milk, and cream to form a custard base, to which flavoring is added. This method produces the richest and smoothest ice creams. Most of the ice cream recipes in this book begin with a traditional custard-type French Vanilla Ice Cream Base (see page 13).

BERRY SYRUP ICE CREAM

This is a still-frozen (unchurned) custard-based ice cream. Still-frozen ice creams are not as creamy as churned ice creams.

> 8 large egg yolks
> 2 cups whipping cream
> 2 cups Fresh Berry Syrup
> (see page 26)
> Dash of salt
> 2 tablespoons sugar, or to taste

1. Combine egg yolks and cream in the top of a double boiler. Place over gently simmering water and cook, stirring constantly, until custard coats the back of a spoon. Remove from heat and cool completely.

2. Stir in Berry Syrup, salt, and sugar. Blend well. Pour into large freezer tray or shallow pan. Cover and freeze ice cream until firm but not hard (2 to 4 hours).

Makes about 1 quart.

PHILADELPHIA-STYLE ICE CREAM

Philadelphia-style ice creams are uncooked. Some use no eggs whatsoever; others use whole eggs. Uncooked ice creams usually have a slightly grainier texture than custard-based ice creams because they lack the emulsifying action of cooked egg yolks that keeps water molecules separated as they freeze. However, bulky flavoring agents, such as significant quantities of fruit pulp or chocolate, can provide their own emulsifying action and make up for the lack of cooked egg yolks, greatly improving the texture of uncooked ice creams.

PHILADELPHIA-STYLE VANILLA ICE CREAM

Adding a whole egg to this recipe will give the ice cream a smoother texture.

> 2 cups whipping cream
> 2 cups half-and-half
> ¾ cup sugar
> 2 teaspoons vanilla extract

1. Mix all ingredients together, stirring until sugar is dissolved.

2. Transfer to an ice cream machine and freeze according to manufacturer's instructions.

Makes about 1 quart.

PHILADELPHIA-STYLE CHOCOLATE ICE CREAM

Chocolate acts as a smoothing agent to give this ice cream a velvet texture.

> 8 ounces semisweet chocolate
> ½ cup sugar
> 1 quart half-and-half
> Pinch of salt

1. In the top of a double boiler over low heat, melt chocolate. Set aside.

2. Combine sugar, half-and-half, and salt. Stir until sugar is completely dissolved. Add melted chocolate, stirring until well mixed.

3. Transfer to an ice cream machine and freeze according to manufacturer's instructions.

Makes about 1 quart.

FRENCH VANILLA ICE CREAM BASE I

This recipe is recommended as the foundation for most of the ice creams in this book. It produces consistently excellent flavor and texture. The same ingredients combined in different proportions give somewhat different results. For example, increasing the milk to 2 cups and reducing the cream to 2 cups will produce a slightly lighter ice cream; adding 2 more egg yolks will make the ice cream richer. Experiment to find which combination of ingredients is most appealing to your palate. Vanilla beans will give a richer flavor than extract. See All About Vanilla and Chocolate, page 18.

> 3 cups whipping cream
> 1 cup milk
> ¾ cup sugar
> 1 vanilla bean, split lengthwise, or 1 tablespoon vanilla extract
> 4 large egg yolks

1. In a heavy-bottomed 2-quart saucepan, heat cream, milk, sugar, and vanilla bean. (If you are using vanilla extract, do not add it until step 4.) Stir occasionally until sugar is dissolved and the mixture is hot but not boiling.

2. Whisk egg yolks together in a bowl. Continue whisking and very slowly pour in approximately 1 cup of the cream mixture. When smooth, pour back into the pan.

3. Whisk constantly over low heat until the mixture thickens slightly and coats the back of a spoon (about 5 minutes). Take care that the mixture doesn't boil, or it will curdle. Draw your finger across the back of the coated spoon. If the line you make remains, the custard is done.

4. Remove vanilla bean; or, if you're using vanilla extract, add it now.

Makes about 1 quart.

French Vanilla Ice Cream Base II Increase vanilla in the above recipe to 2 vanilla beans or 2 tablespoons vanilla extract.

THE STAGES OF WHIPPED CREAM

Always be sure both the cream and the bowl are cold before whipping.

Chantilly stage *The cream falls from the beaters in loose mounds.*

Soft peak stage *When the beaters are lifted, the cream forms downy peaks that collapse within seconds.*

Stiff peak stage *The beaters leave a path in the cream. When the beaters are lifted, the cream forms firm peaks that hold their shape.*

GELATO

Italian gelato contains less air than most French or American ice creams, making it denser and firmer. The Donvier-type ice cream machine makes gelato-like ice cream because it does not incorporate much air into the base during freezing. Use any recipe with French Vanilla Ice Cream Base (see pages 22 to 25). For even richer ice cream, add as many egg yolks as your heart can handle.

FROZEN YOGURT

Frozen yogurt is very similar to ice cream in texture. Yogurt, which is fermented milk, has a rich, slightly acidic taste that combines well with fruit. Frozen yogurt has recently soared in popularity as a low-calorie alternative to ice cream. Any type of yogurt can be used to make frozen yogurt, but one with a higher fat content will give a creamier result.

LEMON FROZEN YOGURT

The combined acidic flavors of yogurt and lemon make this an especially refreshing dessert.

- 4 tablespoons sugar
- 4 containers (8 oz each) lemon-flavored yogurt
  Grated zest of 2 lemons, finely chopped

1. In a mixing bowl whisk sugar into yogurt until completely dissolved (about 2 minutes). Stir in lemon zest.

2. Transfer to an ice cream machine and freeze according to manufacturer's instructions.

Makes about 1 quart.

YOGURT ICE CREAM

Add plain yogurt to French custard to make a tangy ice cream. Fresh fruit can be stirred into the ice cream just before serving.

- 1 cup milk
- 3 large egg yolks
- ½ cup sugar
- 2 cups plain yogurt
- 1 teaspoon vanilla extract

1. Warm milk in a 1-quart saucepan over low heat. Meanwhile, in a 1-quart mixing bowl, beat egg yolks and sugar. When milk forms small bubbles around the edge of the pan, quickly remove from heat and stir thoroughly into egg mixture.

2. Return mixture to saucepan and cook over low heat, stirring constantly, until thick. Be careful not to boil mixture; the eggs will curdle and the milk may scorch. When mixture coats a metal or wooden spoon and a line drawn through it with your finger remains, it is done.

3. Strain into a clean bowl and cool thoroughly. Stir in yogurt and vanilla. Transfer to an ice cream machine and freeze according to manufacturer's instructions.

Makes about 1 quart.

SORBET

Sorbet, sometimes known as sherbet, is a water ice. It is usually made from pulverized fruit pulp, fruit juice, and sugar syrup. You may also see it called *sorbetto* (its Italian name), ice, water ice, Italian ice, or fruit ice. In certain parts of the United States, sherbet contains milk or cream and is technically a milk ice. In those places water ices are usually called sorbets.

The density of the sugar syrup used greatly affects the texture and flavor of a sorbet. French sorbets, made with a fairly light syrup, are slightly grainy and have an intense fruit flavor. Italian sorbettos, made with a heavier syrup, are smoother and sweeter.

SIMPLE SUGAR SYRUP

This traditional syrup falls somewhere between French and Italian. It may be stored in the refrigerator for several weeks.

    2 cups sugar
    1 cup water

1. In a medium-sized saucepan over high heat, cook sugar and the water, stirring constantly, until sugar dissolves and mixture reaches a full, rolling boil.

2. Immediately remove from heat and cool to room temperature. Strain through a fine sieve into a jar or bowl. Cover and refrigerate until needed. Sugar syrup should always be well cooled (to about 40° F) before being used.

Makes about 3 cups.

STRAWBERRY SORBET

This excellent sorbet stores well for up to two weeks.

    2 pints fresh strawberries or
       12 ounces frozen straw-
       berries, without syrup
    1 cup Simple Sugar Syrup
       (at left)
       Juice of ½ lemon

1. Wash and hull strawberries. Purée with Simple Sugar Syrup and lemon juice in a food processor or blender until evenly mixed.

2. Transfer to an ice cream machine and freeze according to manufacturer's instructions.

Makes about 1 quart.

Variation Any fruit that yields a good deal of pulp when puréed may be substituted for strawberries. Other berries, peaches, pears, plums, and melons all give excellent results. Strain raspberry, blackberry, or boysenberry purée through cheesecloth or a fine sieve to remove the seeds. Avoid grinding the seeds against the sieve, as this will cloud both the color and the flavor of the sorbet.

Fresh fruits such as peaches and raspberries make super sorbets. Serve two or three flavors together for a memorable dessert.

15

THE STAGES OF COOKED SUGAR SYRUP

Simple syrup *The sugar has dissolved. The syrup is clear and registers about 215° F on a candy thermometer.*

Soft-ball stage *234° to 240° F. A small spoonful of syrup dropped into ice water then rubbed between finger and thumb forms a soft ball.*

Caramel stage *320° to 355° F. The syrup turns golden brown.*

FRESH LEMON SORBET

When fruits that produce much juice but little pulp—such as lemons, oranges, grapefruit, and other citrus fruits—are used in sorbet, the texture may become grainy because of the greater proportion of liquids to solids. The same is true of sorbets made from sparkling wines, wines, and liqueurs. Adding stiffly beaten egg whites to the sugar syrup base smooths the texture. The syrup base in such sherbets is called an Italian meringue. (For alternative technique see Note below.)

> 2 *large egg whites*
> 2¼ *cups sugar*
> 1 *cup water*
> 1½ *cups freshly squeezed lemon juice*

1. In a large mixing bowl beat egg whites until very stiff. Set aside.

2. In a medium-sized saucepan over high heat, cook sugar and the water, stirring constantly, until sugar dissolves and mixture reaches a full, rolling boil. Remove from heat and slowly drizzle hot syrup into egg whites, whisking constantly until all the syrup is incorporated. Continue whisking and slowly add lemon juice. Stir over an ice-water bath or cover and refrigerate until cold.

3. Transfer to an ice cream machine and freeze according to manufacturer's instructions.

Makes about 1 quart.

Note Another technique for improving the texture of sorbets with a high liquids-to-solids ratio is to increase the proportion of sugar syrup to 50 percent of the total volume of the mixture. The extra sugar helps to minimize the size of the ice crystals that form during freezing.

ICE MILK

Ice milk, also called milk ice or cream ice, has less butterfat and a lighter texture than ice cream. It is actually sorbet to which a small amount of milk or cream has been added. This hybrid of ice cream and sorbet originated in Arabia, where it is called *sharbah*. The word may be the source of the English word *sherbet*.

Although commonly thought to be a low-calorie alternative to ice cream, some ice milks contain up to twice the sugar of some ice creams and therefore have more calories. To improve its texture, commercially made ice milk often contains large quantities of air and has more artificial stabilizers and emulsifiers added than ice cream.

GRANITA

Granita is sorbet that is frozen without constant churning. The name *granita* is Spanish and refers to the grainy, granular texture of this dessert. In general granitas have less sugar than sorbets. They should be served slightly thawed and slushy. If granitas are whipped in a blender or a food processor with a metal blade just before being served, the resulting texture is nearly as smooth as that of a churned sorbet.

WHITE ZINFANDEL GRANITA

Any dry white wine will work in this refreshing granita.

> 1½ *cups water*
> ¾ *cup sugar*
> 1½ *cups white Zinfandel*

1. In a medium-sized saucepan bring the water, sugar, and ¾ cup of the wine to a boil, stirring constantly until sugar dissolves. Reduce heat and simmer for 3 minutes without stirring.

2. Allow syrup to cool to room temperature or cool in refrigerator. Add remaining wine to cooled syrup. Pour into a shallow metal pan and place in freezer compartment of refrigerator.

3. Freeze until firm (1½ to 2 hours), stirring well every 30 minutes. Allow to warm slightly and stir one final time before serving.

Makes about 1 quart.

GRANITA CAFÉ
Use a strong-flavored coffee for best results.

    1 cup water
    ¾ cup sugar
    1 cinnamon stick (about
       3 in. long)
    2 or 3 strips lemon peel
    2 or 3 whole cloves
    3 cups espresso or double-
       strength coffee, chilled

1. In a medium-sized saucepan combine the water, sugar, cinnamon stick, lemon peel, and cloves. Bring to a boil, stirring constantly until sugar dissolves. Reduce heat and simmer slowly without stirring for 4 minutes.

2. Remove from heat; discard cinnamon stick, lemon peel, and cloves. Cool to room temperature. Stir in coffee. Pour into a shallow metal pan and place in freezer compartment of refrigerator.

3. Freeze until firm (1½ to 2 hours), stirring well every 30 minutes. Allow to warm slightly and stir one final time before serving.

Makes about 1 quart.

End a zesty Italian meal with a not-too-sweet coffee-flavored granita, served with your favorite homemade or storebought cookies. For the recipe for the Almond–Poppy Seed Cookies above, see the California Culinary Academy book Cookies.

17

ALL ABOUT VANILLA AND CHOCOLATE

The two best-loved ice cream flavors in the United States are chocolate and vanilla. Both are derived from beans that grow and develop their rich, satisfying flavors in tropical climates.

VANILLA

The vanilla bean is the pod of an orchid native to Central America. When ripe and ready for hand-picking, the pod is yellow and odorless. Its characteristic aroma and dark color develop during a slow sunning and drying period. A whole commercial vanilla bean is generally 4 to 5 inches long and chocolate brown. Slit open lengthwise, the pod reveals hundreds of minuscule black seeds; these are the specks visible in many high-quality vanilla ice creams.

Vanilla is prized for the flavor it imparts to dishes, primarily sweets. It is the most popular ice cream flavor in America, and it has an affinity for other custard desserts as well. It is often paired with chocolate, as it heightens the chocolate flavor.

Buying Vanilla

Whole vanilla beans are available on most supermarket spice shelves and from specialty stores. All supermarkets carry bottled pure vanilla extract and imitation vanilla extract. Pure extract is more expensive but far superior in flavor.

Whole vanilla beans should be pliable and have a fine white bloom of vanillin crystals on the outside. Avoid beans that are excessively hard and dry. Vanilla beans can be stored for several months in a tightly covered jar in a cool place. The best pure vanilla extract has a rich, well-balanced aroma and flavor. Store vanilla extract in a cool, dark place; it keeps well for up to a year.

Working With Vanilla

Like all alcohol-based extracts, vanilla extract is highly volatile (its flavor dissipates when it is exposed to air and heat). For maximum effect add it to cool or cooling liquids. Whole vanilla beans can be added to a sauce or simmering liquid, then strained out. Rinsed and dried, the bean can be reused. More often, vanilla beans are split lengthwise and their seeds scraped into the simmering liquid.

Vanilla Sugar

When either granulated or confectioners' sugar is infused with the flavor and perfume of the vanilla bean, the result is a delicious product that can be substituted for plain sugar in any recipe.

Split a vanilla bean in half lengthwise. Place both halves in a tall jar. Fill jar with 1 to 2 cups granulated or confectioners' sugar. Cover and let stand for at least 24 hours to allow sugar to absorb vanilla flavor. Replenish sugar as you use it. Vanilla will continue to flavor sugar for up to a year. Stirring may dislodge some of the tiny seeds inside the split vanilla bean. They will add a potent flavor as they become distributed throughout the sugar. If these tiny specks become too numerous, strain sugar through a fine sieve as you use it, returning seeds to jar.

CHOCOLATE

Chocolate is produced from cocoa beans, the seeds of the tropical cocoa (or cacao) tree. The seeds themselves are quite bitter; although the Aztecs enjoyed a beverage made from roasted, ground cocoa beans mixed with hot water, today's tastes demand further processing. Numerous advances in processing have led to a variety of chocolate products, ranging from unsweetened cocoa to milk chocolate.

The processing of chocolate begins with the harvest of the pods of the cocoa tree. Pods are broken open and the seeds and pulp removed. The seeds are allowed to ferment for two to nine days to develop flavor; they are then dried, graded, packed, and shipped. The chocolate manufacturer generally blends seeds from several sources to produce a consistent style and desirable flavor. After cleaning and blending the seeds, the manufacturer roasts them to develop flavor and aroma. After roasting and cooling, the seeds are shelled. The meat, or nibs, are saved; the shells are sold for animal feed or fertilizer. The nibs, which are slightly more than 50 percent cocoa butter, are then ground to produce chocolate liquor.

Types of Chocolate

Solid unsweetened chocolate is made by pouring chocolate liquor into molds and letting it solidify. "Eating chocolate" has cocoa butter and sugar added to the chocolate liquor. Distinctions of bittersweet, semisweet, and sweet do not correspond to any fixed degree of sweetness; the amount of sugar in each depends on the formula of the individual manufacturer.

According to U.S. Food and Drug Administration regulations, sweet chocolate may contain less than half the chocolate liquor required in bittersweet chocolate.

Although different manufacturers use different formulations, bittersweet chocolate is usually the most intensely chocolate flavored and the least sweet, with semisweet chocolate being sweeter, and sweet chocolate being sweeter still. The three are usually interchangeable in recipes.

Milk chocolate is made by adding dried milk solids to sweetened chocolate. It is widely used for candy bars and other confections but is rarely used in cooking. It should not be used in recipes unless specified.

White chocolate is not technically chocolate at all because it lacks chocolate liquor. White chocolate is cocoa butter with added sugar, milk, and flavorings. It may contain lecithin, and it usually contains vanilla or vanillin. It should not be substituted for chocolate in recipes.

Buying Chocolate

Unsweetened chocolate is usually sold in 8-ounce boxes, with the chocolate divided into tissue-wrapped 1-ounce squares for easy measuring.

Most bittersweet, semisweet, and sweet chocolate is sold in paper-wrapped bars. Semisweet chocolate is also made into chips and packed in bags; chips may be substituted for semisweet chocolate bars ounce for ounce. Semisweet chips, however, usually have a lower cocoa butter content than semisweet chocolate bars; thus their flavor is less intense, and they melt less easily.

Cocoa and instant cocoa are generally packed in airtight tins.

Storing Chocolate

Keep solid chocolate wrapped airtight in a cool, dry place; it stores well for up to four months. Chocolate kept in the refrigerator will sweat when brought to room temperature and may not melt properly. Chocolate stored in a warm place may develop bloom, a dusty white coating caused by melted cocoa butter rising to the surface. The bloom is harmless, and the chocolate may safely be used. Cocoa will keep indefinitely in an airtight tin in a cool place.

Working With Chocolate

Chocolate is temperamental. It burns easily and should always be melted slowly. When melting chocolate by itself for any purpose, it is best to chop it into small pieces. Place chopped chocolate in the top of a double boiler or in a stainless steel bowl over a pan of hot (not boiling) water; adjust heat so water remains just below a simmer. Take care not to let water boil or allow steam to rise and settle in the pan of chocolate. If there is a speck of water in the container used to melt the chocolate, the chocolate will seize (tighten) into an unmeltable mass. To salvage seized chocolate stir in 1 teaspoon of vegetable shortening per ounce of chocolate.

Chocolate will melt well in liquid (such as milk or cream) as long as there is at least 1 tablespoon of liquid per ounce of chocolate. Chocolate can also be melted in a microwave oven. Put chocolate in a glass container and set oven on medium or high heat; chocolate will melt in 1 to 3 minutes, depending on its volume.

Bring back the fun of the past with homemade soda fountain treats. Mix and match ice creams and toppings to produce your personal hit parade of sundaes.

From the Soda Fountain

The soda fountain is part of the vanishing memory of early twentieth-century America. The black and white checkered floors, the marble counters, the snappy lingo of the soda jerk (in which "burn one all the way" meant a chocolate malted with chocolate ice cream and chocolate syrup) are all rapidly disappearing. Although finding an authentic soda fountain today may be difficult, duplicating its wonderful excesses at home is both easy and fun. With very little effort, you can make your own marvelous milkshakes (see page 36), fabulous frappes (see page 36), and sensational sundaes and sodas (see pages 39 and 35).

HOMEMADE ICE CREAM

Ice cream is the foundation for most soda fountain treats. Homemade, it has a fresh, natural taste rarely achieved in purchased ice creams and a texture that is particularly rich, creamy, and satisfying. One great advantage of making your own ice cream is that you can choose the recipe that gives exactly the richness and creaminess desired (see French Vanilla Ice Cream Base I and II, page 13). You can also select the flavor intensity. For example, if you are an ardent vanilla lover, you can increase the amount of vanilla in a recipe; if you're a chocoholic, you can go heavy on the chocolate.

The following recipes re-create some of the most popular soda fountain ice cream flavors and add a few new ones. Enjoy them alone or as elements in the more elaborate desserts that begin on page 35.

CHOCOLATE ICE CREAM

This ice cream is a rich treat for chocolate lovers.

3 ounces semisweet chocolate
1 ounce unsweetened chocolate
1 recipe French Vanilla Ice Cream Base I (see page 13)

1. Melt the chocolates together slowly in a double boiler. Meanwhile, prepare French Vanilla Ice Cream Base I.

2. Slowly add ½ cup of warm ice cream base to melted chocolate, whisking constantly to keep chocolate smooth. Return mixture to ice cream base, mix well, and let cool.

3. Transfer to an ice cream machine and freeze according to manufacturer's instructions.

Makes about 1 quart.

FRENCH VANILLA ICE CREAM

True ice cream aficionados always return to the rich flavor of vanilla ice cream.

1 recipe French Vanilla Ice Cream Base II (see page 13)

1. Prepare French Vanilla Ice Cream Base II.

2. Strain into a clean bowl and cool thoroughly.

3. Transfer to an ice cream machine and freeze according to manufacturer's instructions.

Makes about 1 quart.

STRAWBERRY ICE CREAM

Use plump, ripe strawberries to make the most of this summertime favorite.

1 recipe French Vanilla Ice Cream Base II (see page 13)
2 pints strawberries
½ cup sugar, or to taste

1. Prepare French Vanilla Ice Cream Base II. Strain into a clean bowl and cool thoroughly.

2. Wash and hull strawberries. In a large bowl mash berries; add sugar and let stand for 1 hour. (Use more sugar if the berries are not sweet, less if they are very sweet.) Add strawberries to strained ice cream base.

3. Transfer to an ice cream machine and freeze according to manufacturer's instructions.

Makes 1 quart.

CHOCOLATE CHIP ICE CREAM

This ice cream is a happy combination of two of the world's most popular flavors: chocolate and vanilla.

1 recipe French Vanilla Ice Cream Base II (see page 13)
1 cup miniature chocolate chips

1. Prepare French Vanilla Ice Cream Base II. Strain into a clean bowl and cool thoroughly.

2. Transfer to an ice cream machine and freeze according to manufacturer's instructions, adding chocolate chips halfway through freezing.

Makes about 1 quart.

ROCKY ROAD ICE CREAM

This dark and crunchy ice cream will make life's roads easier to travel.

1 recipe Dark Chocolate Ice Cream (see page 39)
1 cup miniature marshmallows
1 cup toasted walnuts, chopped (see Note)

Prepare Dark Chocolate Ice Cream. When freezing process is almost complete, add marshmallows and walnuts, mixing well. Complete freezing process.

Makes about 1 quart.

Note To toast nuts: Preheat oven to 350° F. Spread nuts in a single layer in a baking pan. Toast 5 to 10 minutes or until nuts are lightly browned and fragrant. Watch them carefully; they burn easily.

COFFEE ICE CREAM

A must for lovers of the fragrant coffee bean.

1 recipe French Vanilla Ice Cream Base II (see page 13)
2 tablespoons instant espresso powder

1. Prepare French Vanilla Ice Cream Base II. Add espresso powder and whisk until dissolved.

2. Strain into a clean bowl and cool thoroughly.

3. Transfer to an ice cream machine and freeze according to manufacturer's instructions.

Makes about 1 quart.

MAPLE-WALNUT ICE CREAM

The better the maple syrup, the better the flavor of the ice cream.

1 recipe French Vanilla Ice Cream Base II (see page 13), without sugar
¾ cup pure maple syrup
1 cup toasted walnuts, chopped (see Rocky Road Ice Cream, Note, page 22)

1. Prepare French Vanilla Ice Cream Base II using maple syrup instead of sugar. Strain into a clean bowl and cool thoroughly.

2. Transfer to an ice cream machine and begin to freeze according to manufacturer's instructions. Midway through freezing process, add walnuts. Complete freezing.

Makes about 1 quart.

PEPPERMINT-STICK ICE CREAM

This is a favorite among children, perhaps because it is the color of bubble gum.

4 ounces (about ½ cup) hard peppermint candies
1 recipe French Vanilla Ice Cream Base II (see page 13)
1 teaspoon peppermint extract

1. Crush peppermint candies into small pieces by wrapping them in a paper towel and hitting them with a mallet.

2. Prepare French Vanilla Ice Cream Base II. Strain into a clean bowl. Add crushed candies and peppermint extract, mixing well. The candies will partially melt, turning the ice cream peppermint pink.

3. Transfer to an ice cream machine and freeze according to manufacturer's instructions.

Makes about 1 quart.

There's something for everybody when you offer an array of luscious home-made ice creams in a decorative serving bowl. Arrange the scoops well in advance, then cover and freeze until serving time.

HOW TO MAKE RIPPLES

The secret to making a perfect ripple effect is to use a syrup or sauce with a rather thick consistency. A very thin syrup would result in a not very well defined ripple.

1. *Use ice cream directly from the ice cream machine; it will still be soft. Spread 1 inch of ice cream in the bottom of the container to be used for freezing.*

2. *On top of the ice cream, spread a thin layer of the sauce that will form the ripples.*

3. *Alternate layers of ice cream and sauce until the container is full.*

4. *With a wooden spoon or sturdy pastry spatula, cut straight down through the center of the ice cream.*

5. *Pull the utensil through the mixture from side to side two or three times, then remove it by pulling straight up. Place ice cream in the freezer to firm up (about 1 hour).*

FUDGE RIPPLE ICE CREAM

Perfect your rippling technique with this popular ice cream, then create flavor combinations of your own.

    6 ounces bittersweet chocolate
    3 tablespoons unsalted butter
    ½ cup sugar
    1 cup milk
    2 tablespoons light corn syrup
    1 teaspoon vanilla extract
    1 recipe French Vanilla
      Ice Cream (see page 22)

1. In the top of a double boiler, melt chocolate and butter, stirring until mixture is completely smooth.

2. Cook sugar and milk in a small saucepan over low heat until sugar is dissolved. Stir in chocolate mixture and corn syrup. Continue cooking for about 5 minutes, stirring constantly. Remove from heat and stir in vanilla. Refrigerate at least 2 hours before using in ice cream.

3. Layer ice cream with sauce, and ripple as shown at left.

Makes about 1 quart.

Chocolate-Raspberry Ripple
Combine Chocolate-Raspberry Sauce (see page 28) and Chocolate Ice Cream (see page 22).

Strawberry Ripple Combine Strawberry Sauce (see page 42) and French Vanilla Ice Cream (see page 22).

Peanut Butter–Fudge Ripple
Combine Old-Fashioned Chocolate Sauce (see page 30) and Peanut Butter Ice Cream (see page 25).

Butter Pecan–Butterscotch Ripple Combine Old-Fashioned Butterscotch Sauce (see page 30) and Butter Pecan Ice Cream (see page 42).

FRESH FRUIT ICE CREAM

This flavorful ice cream combines three of summer's most bountiful fruits. To make individual fruit-flavored ice creams (such as peach, banana, or blueberry) simply use 4 cups of the fruit of your choice in place of the mixed fruit.

>   4 cups fresh, mixed fruit: peaches, nectarines, and apricots
>   ¼ to ½ cup sugar, or to taste
>   1 recipe French Vanilla Ice Cream Base II (see page 13)

1. Peel, stone, chop, and mash fruit. Stir in sugar (less if fruit is very sweet, more if it is not sweet enough) and let stand for 1 hour.

2. Prepare French Vanilla Ice Cream Base II. Strain into a clean bowl and stir in fruit. Cool thoroughly.

3. Transfer to an ice cream machine and freeze according to manufacturer's instructions.

Makes about 1 quart.

RUM-RAISIN ICE CREAM

A high-quality dark rum makes all the difference in the flavor of this ice cream.

>   ½ cup raisins
>   3 ounces dark rum
>   1 recipe French Vanilla Ice Cream Base II (see page 13)

1. Soak raisins in rum for at least 1 hour.

2. Prepare French Vanilla Ice Cream Base II. Strain into a clean bowl and cool thoroughly.

3. Transfer to an ice cream machine and begin freezing according to manufacturer's instructions. Midway through freezing process, add raisin-rum mixture. Complete freezing.

Makes about 1 quart.

PEANUT BUTTER ICE CREAM

The rich flavor of peanuts and the smoothness of vanilla ice cream make this an unexpected delight.

>   1 cup smooth or chunky peanut butter
>   1 recipe French Vanilla Ice Cream Base II (see page 13)

1. In a small, heavy-bottomed saucepan, melt peanut butter over low heat. Set aside. Prepare French Vanilla Ice Cream Base II. Strain into a clean bowl, add melted peanut butter, and mix well. Cool thoroughly.

2. Transfer to an ice cream machine and freeze according to manufacturer's instructions.

Makes about 1 quart.

BURNT-SUGAR ICE CREAM

The caramel flavor of this rich ice cream appeals to all ages.

>   1½ cups sugar
>   3 cups whipping cream
>   8 large egg yolks
>   1 cup milk

1. In a heavy-bottomed 2-quart saucepan, cook sugar over high heat, stirring occasionally, until it melts and is copper colored.

2. Immediately pour in cream in a steady stream, taking care that mixture does not bubble over. The cream will harden the sugar. Continue to cook over medium heat, stirring, until sugar melts again.

3. In a small bowl whisk together egg yolks and milk. Add a ladleful of hot sugar mixture to yolks, whisking constantly. Then pour yolks into sugar mixture, whisking to keep eggs from cooking too fast.

4. Cook mixture over medium heat, whisking constantly, until it is thick enough to coat the back of a spoon (see French Vanilla Ice Cream Base I, step 3, page 13). Strain into a clean bowl and cool thoroughly.

5. Transfer to an ice cream machine and freeze according to manufacturer's instructions.

Makes about 1 quart.

SYRUPS

Flavored syrups are easily made and can be stored in the refrigerator for months. They can be used to flavor sodas (see page 35) and milkshakes (see page 36); to top elaborate sundaes (see page 39), parfaits (see page 42), and banana splits (see page 40); or to add a splash of contrasting flavor to a single scoop of ice cream. They give the amateur soda jerk extra flexibility and flair, and an easy way of intensifying favorite flavors (try using *both* strawberry syrup and strawberry sauce on your next strawberry sundae). Syrups also work wonders with pancakes and waffles, turn plain carbonated water into a refreshing cooler, and add a new flavor dimension to poached fruits. In addition to the syrup recipes that follow, see Ginger Syrup (page 35) and Pineapple Syrup (page 36).

BASIC NUT SYRUP

This syrup is great on pancakes and waffles as well as ice cream.

>   2 cups sugar
>   ¾ cup water
>   ¼ cup dark corn syrup
>   ½ teaspoon vanilla extract
>   1 cup toasted, coarsely chopped nuts, such as walnuts, pecans, almonds, hazelnuts, or unsalted peanuts (see Rocky Road Ice Cream, Note, page 22)

1. In a small, heavy-bottomed saucepan, combine sugar, the water, and corn syrup. Stir over medium heat until sugar dissolves. Raise heat and boil gently until mixture thickens to desired syrup consistency (2 to 3 minutes).

2. Remove from heat. Add vanilla and nuts. Refrigerate until needed.

Makes about 2½ cups.

With a choice of homemade syrups and ice creams, this easily made "waffle à la mode" can become your signature dessert.

COFFEE SYRUP

This syrup has a rich coffee taste and aroma to perk up your taste buds.

> ½ cup firmly packed light
>   brown sugar
> 2 tablespoons dark corn syrup
> ½ cup water
> 1 tablespoon instant
>   espresso powder

1. In a small, heavy-bottomed saucepan, combine sugar, corn syrup, and the water. Bring to a boil and cook over medium heat, stirring constantly, until sugar is dissolved.

2. Remove from heat. Add espresso powder, stirring until it is dissolved. Skim any froth that forms. Cool to room temperature, then refrigerate until needed.

Makes about 1 cup.

FRESH BERRY SYRUP

Take advantage of whatever berries are at their peak of sweetness.

> 4 cups fresh berries, such as
>   strawberries, raspberries,
>   blueberries, or blackberries,
>   or a combination
> 1 cup sugar
> 1 cup water

1. Hull and clean berries if necessary. In a 2-quart saucepan combine berries, sugar, and the water. Bring to a boil, stirring and washing down sides of pan with a pastry brush dipped in cold water. When sugar is dissolved simmer mixture 10 minutes without stirring.

2. Cool to lukewarm and strain through a fine sieve into a jar, pressing hard to extract all the liquid. Chill thoroughly before using.

Makes about 2½ cups.

BITTERSWEET CHOCOLATE SYRUP

The chocolate flavor of this syrup is deep, dark, and not too sweet.

> ½ cup water
> ½ cup unsweetened
>   cocoa powder
> ½ cup sugar
> 1 teaspoon vanilla extract

1. In a small, heavy-bottomed saucepan, combine the water, cocoa, and sugar. Cook over medium heat, stirring constantly, until cocoa and sugar are dissolved and mixture is smooth.

2. Remove from heat, stir in vanilla, and let cool. Refrigerate until needed.

Makes about 1 cup.

LEMON SYRUP

This syrup is also a terrific base for lemonade.

>   1 cup fresh lemon juice (about 8 medium lemons)
>   1 cup sugar
>   Zest of 2 lemons, finely chopped

1. Combine lemon juice, sugar, and zest in a small saucepan. Bring to a boil over medium heat, stirring and washing down sides of pan with a pastry brush dipped in cold water. When sugar is dissolved simmer mixture about 10 minutes without stirring.

2. Remove from heat, cool to luke-warm, and strain through a fine sieve into a jar. Refrigerate until needed.

Makes about 1 cup.

LIME SYRUP

Try this when fresh limes are bountiful.

>   1 cup fresh lime juice (about 12 limes)
>   1 cup sugar
>   Zest of 4 limes, finely chopped

Proceed as for Lemon Syrup (above).

Makes about 1 cup.

ORANGE SYRUP

This is a tangy syrup, great for brightening up drinks.

>   1 cup fresh orange juice (about 4 medium oranges)
>   ½ cup sugar
>   Zest of 1 orange, finely chopped

Proceed as for Lemon Syrup (above).

Makes about 1 cup.

PEACH SYRUP

Preserve the luscious flavor of summer's peaches in this tasty syrup.

>   3 pounds peaches, peeled, stoned, and chopped
>   1 cup sugar
>   ½ cup water

1. In a food processor fitted with a steel blade, purée peaches. In a 2-quart saucepan combine purée with sugar and the water. Bring to a boil over medium heat, stirring and washing down sides of pan with a pastry brush dipped in cold water. When sugar is dissolved simmer mixture 10 minutes without stirring.

2. Remove from heat, cool to luke-warm, and strain through a fine sieve into a jar, pressing hard to extract all the liquid. Refrigerate until needed.

Makes about 2 cups.

SWEET CHOCOLATE SYRUP

This syrup is an excellent base for chocolate sodas and milkshakes.

>   ½ cup water
>   ½ cup unsweetened cocoa powder
>   ½ cup sugar
>   ½ cup light corn syrup
>   1 teaspoon vanilla extract

1. In a small, heavy-bottomed saucepan, combine the water, cocoa, and sugar. Cook over medium heat, stirring constantly, until cocoa and sugar are dissolved and mixture is smooth.

2. Remove from heat, stir in corn syrup and vanilla, and let cool. Refrigerate until needed.

Makes about 1½ cups.

TOPPINGS

Toppings for ice cream desserts run the gamut from simple crushed fruit (see page 33) to such fabulous, rich creations as Almond-Raisin Fudge Sauce (below). For adults, spirited toppings, such as Chocolate-Rum Sauce (see page 28), are always popular. For a quick dessert for children, you can simply sprinkle crushed cookies over a scoop of ice cream. The toppings in this chapter can be made ahead of time, making it easy to incorporate old-fashioned soda fountain treats into a busy day. In addition to the recipes that follow, see Bourbon-Pecan Sauce (page 39), Hot Fudge Sauce (page 42), and Peppermint Sauce (page 39).

ALMOND-RAISIN FUDGE SAUCE

Toasting the nuts helps bring out their flavor.

>   ¼ cup unsalted butter
>   2 ounces unsweetened chocolate
>   ¼ cup unsweetened cocoa powder
>   ¾ cup sugar
>   ⅔ cup whipping cream
>   Pinch of salt
>   1 teaspoon vanilla extract
>   ½ cup raisins, coarsely chopped
>   ¼ cup chopped or slivered almonds, toasted (see Rocky Road Ice Cream, Note, page 22)

In a heavy-bottomed 1-quart saucepan, melt butter and chocolate over low heat. Stir in cocoa, sugar, cream, and salt. Bring slowly to a boil. Remove from heat and add vanilla, raisins, and almonds. Serve warm or at room temperature.

Makes about 1½ cups.

BUTTERSCOTCH-PECAN SAUCE

Other nuts may be substituted for the pecans in this rich and flavorful sauce. Use your favorites.

2 tablespoons unsalted butter
⅓ cup chopped pecans
½ cup dark corn syrup
½ cup firmly packed dark brown sugar
¼ cup whipping cream
1 teaspoon vanilla extract

1. In a small skillet melt butter over medium heat. Add pecans and sauté until nuts turn golden brown.

2. In a medium-sized saucepan combine corn syrup, brown sugar, and cream. Cook over medium heat about 5 minutes, stirring occasionally. Add vanilla and sautéed nuts. Remove from heat. Serve hot or cold.

Makes about 2 cups.

CHOCOLATE-RASPBERRY SAUCE

This is one instance in which frozen berries are better than fresh.

1 package (10 oz) raspberries frozen in syrup
¼ cup sugar
5 ounces semisweet chocolate, chopped into ½-inch pieces
2 tablespoons unsalted butter, softened

1. Thaw raspberries in their syrup. Mash berries to a mushlike consistency.

2. In a heavy-bottomed 1-quart saucepan, bring sugar and berries to a boil. Add chocolate and butter and cook, stirring constantly, until melted.

3. Serve hot, or cool to room temperature and refrigerate. Sauce will keep for several weeks. To use, reheat over hot water.

Makes about 1¼ cups.

CHOCOLATE-RUM SAUCE

Dark rum gives a sweeter, deeper flavor than would its paler counterpart.

1 cup whipping cream
¼ cup sugar
4 ounces semisweet chocolate, chopped
2 ounces unsweetened chocolate, chopped
3 tablespoons unsalted butter
¼ cup dark rum

1. Cook cream in a heavy-bottomed 2-quart saucepan over medium heat until it is reduced by about one third its volume (about 5 minutes). Add sugar and stir gently until it just melts.

2. Remove from heat, whisk in both chocolates until completely melted, then whisk in butter. When mixture is smooth, whisk in rum.

Makes about 1½ cups.

MAPLE SAUCE

Use pure maple syrup; imitation maple syrup will not give good results.

1 cup pure maple syrup
½ cup sugar
⅓ cup whipping cream
3 tablespoons unsalted butter
1 tablespoon light corn syrup

1. In a small saucepan combine all ingredients. Cook over high heat, stirring constantly, until butter is melted and sugar is dissolved (about 3 minutes). Reduce heat to medium and cook another 5 minutes.

2. Remove from heat; let cool a few minutes before serving.

Makes about 1 cup.

COFFEE SAUCE

Instant coffee does not have the same flavor intensity as powdered espresso, so use more if you substitute it.

2 tablespoons cornstarch
1 cup plus 2 tablespoons cold water
¾ cup sugar
¾ cup half-and-half
3 tablespoons instant espresso powder
2 teaspoons vanilla extract
Pinch of salt

1. Dissolve cornstarch in 2 tablespoons of the water.

2. In a small, heavy-bottomed saucepan, combine sugar and ¼ cup of the water. Bring to a boil, stirring and washing down sides of pan with a pastry brush dipped in cold tap water. Boil without stirring until mixture reaches a golden caramel color.

3. Remove from heat and very carefully add remaining ¾ cup of the water, stirring until the caramel is dissolved. Stir in cornstarch mixture and cook over medium heat until sauce thickens (a few minutes).

4. Add half-and-half and bring to a boil. Immediately remove from heat and stir in espresso powder, vanilla, and salt. Stir until espresso powder is dissolved.

5. Cool to room temperature, then chill at least 1 hour.

Makes about 2 cups.

CINNAMON-BLUEBERRY SAUCE

Frozen blueberries may be substituted for fresh.

2 cups blueberries
1 tablespoon ground cinnamon
½ cup sugar
8 tablespoons unsalted butter
2 tablespoons lemon juice

In a heavy-bottomed 1-quart saucepan, combine all ingredients. Cook over medium heat until berries break and sauce thickens (about 5 minutes). Serve warm. Sauce can be refrigerated and reheated.

Makes about 1½ cups.

Smooth and velvety or studded with fruit and nuts, home-made toppings offer a temptation few ice cream lovers can resist.

MARSHMALLOW SAUCE

This recipe makes a wonderful, thick, old-fashioned type of marshmallow sauce.

1 tablespoon unflavored gelatin
2 teaspoons cornstarch
½ cup half-and-half
2 large egg whites, at room temperature
Pinch of cream of tartar
Pinch of salt
1 cup sugar
½ cup light corn syrup
½ cup water
2 teaspoons vanilla extract

1. In a small, heavy-bottomed saucepan, combine gelatin, cornstarch, and half-and-half. Let stand 10 minutes, then warm over low heat, stirring until gelatin dissolves. Do not boil. Remove from heat and keep warm while preparing rest of sauce.

2. In the large bowl of an electric mixer, beat egg whites with cream of tartar and salt until soft peaks form (see page 14).

3. In a small, heavy-bottomed saucepan, combine sugar, corn syrup, and the water. Bring to a boil over medium heat, washing down sides of pan with a brush dipped in cold water. Cook without stirring until mixture reaches soft-ball stage (see page 16) or until a candy thermometer reaches about 238° F.

4. Resume beating egg whites. Add the sugar syrup in a steady stream. Add the warm half-and-half mixture and continue beating until the entire mixture is at room temperature. Beat in vanilla. Chill until sauce gels (at least 3 hours).

5. When you're ready to use the sauce, beat it with an electric mixer until it reaches pouring consistency.

Makes about 2 cups.

OLD-FASHIONED BUTTERSCOTCH SAUCE

This sauce is a favorite among butterscotch lovers.

½ cup unsalted butter
1 cup firmly packed light brown sugar
3 tablespoons light corn syrup
½ cup whipping cream

In a small, heavy-bottomed saucepan, melt butter. Stir in brown sugar, corn syrup, and cream. Bring to a boil over medium heat. Remove from heat and cool slightly before serving.

Makes about 1½ cups.

OLD-FASHIONED CHOCOLATE SAUCE

This sauce is the kind your mother might have made, with a slightly grainy texture.

8 ounces bittersweet chocolate
½ cup light corn syrup
½ cup whipping cream
2 teaspoons vanilla extract

In a heavy-bottomed 1-quart saucepan, melt chocolate over low heat. Add corn syrup and stir until smooth. Stir in cream and vanilla. Serve warm or at room temperature.

Makes about 1½ cups.

PINEAPPLE SAUCE

This sweet, aromatic sauce will quickly become a favorite.

1 large pineapple (about 4 lb)
½ cup sugar

1. Peel, core, and chop pineapple. Reserve about 2 cups. In a food processor fitted with a steel blade or in a blender in batches, purée remaining pineapple.

2. In a medium saucepan bring the puréed pineapple and sugar to a boil over medium heat. Simmer, stirring occasionally, about 5 minutes.

3. Strain through a sieve, pressing hard to extract all the liquid. Skim off the froth and add the reserved pineapple. Cover and chill.

Makes about 3 cups.

SPICED PEACH SAUCE

This is a wonderful way to use fruit that is blemished or bruised.

1 pound fully ripe peaches
3 tablespoons lemon juice
1½ cups honey, or to taste
¼ teaspoon each ground ginger and ground allspice, or to taste

1. Peel and pit peaches. Purée in a food processor fitted with a steel blade or in a blender in batches.

2. In a small, heavy-bottomed saucepan over low heat, gently simmer peaches and lemon juice about 5 minutes. Remove from heat; add honey, ginger, and allspice. Mix well. Taste and add more honey or spices if needed.

Makes about 2½ cups.

VANILLA SAUCE

This extremely versatile sauce is delicious as is and lends itself to a number of wonderful variations. It is also good served alongside plain frozen fruits, such as red seedless grapes or persimmons. For the best flavor, use only high-quality vanilla.

½ cup light corn syrup
¼ cup sugar
1½ cups whipping cream
¼ cup unsalted butter
1 tablespoon cornstarch
2 teaspoons vanilla extract

1. In a heavy-bottomed 1-quart saucepan, bring corn syrup, sugar, and cream to a boil. Reduce heat and simmer 2 to 3 minutes, stirring occasionally. Add butter; stir until it is melted and remove from heat.

2. In a small bowl stir together cornstarch and ¼ cup of the corn syrup mixture. When thoroughly incorporated, return to pan. Stir in vanilla.

Makes about 2½ cups.

Berry Vanilla Sauce Add 1 cup fresh raspberries, blueberries, or blackberries to cooled sauce.

Cherry Vanilla Sauce Add ⅓ cup high-quality cherry preserves with the vanilla.

Chocolate Chip Vanilla Sauce Add 1 cup miniature chocolate chips to cooled sauce.

Chutney Vanilla Sauce Add ½ cup chopped mango chutney to cooled sauce. (Try this sauce on Coconut Ice Cream, page 35.)

Cranberry Vanilla Sauce Add ½ cup cranberry sauce to warm sauce; mix well to dissolve.

Honey Vanilla Sauce Add 2 tablespoons honey with the vanilla.

Light Rum Sauce Add 2 tablespoons light rum with the vanilla.

Miss Jane Marble Sauce While sauce is still warm, add 1 cup chocolate chips. Swirl with a fork to make a marbled design.

Peanut Butter Vanilla Sauce While sauce is still warm, add ¼ cup melted peanut butter.

Vanilla-Banana Sauce Add ½ cup ripe mashed bananas and 2 tablespoons dark rum with the vanilla.

Vanilla-Nut Sauce Add 1 cup chopped, toasted nuts to the cooled sauce.

Special Feature

FRENCH BRANDIED FRUITS

Brandied fruits are a wonderful way to use the fruits of the season, adding new ones to the crock as they ripen. Enjoy brandied fruits as the French do, spooned over vanilla ice cream (see Coupes, page 42). Fill a jar from the crock for a special gift any time; everyone loves receiving summer fruits in the dead of winter.

> 9 *cups diced mixed fruit, such as strawberries, blackberries, Bing cherries, pineapple, apricots, peaches, nectarines, seedless grapes, or other seasonal fruits*
> 5 *cups sugar*
> 5 *cups firmly packed light brown sugar*
> 1 *quart brandy*

1. Prepare fruit. Peaches, nectarines, and apricots should be peeled, stoned, and chopped. Pineapple should be peeled, cored, and cubed. Cherries should be pitted. All fruit should be chopped to roughly the same size as the cherries.

2. In a very large bowl combine sugars. Add fruit and toss to coat. Cover the bowl and let stand 1 hour, tossing every 15 minutes.

3. Transfer fruit to a 1½-gallon crock and pour in brandy. Place a plate on top to weight down fruit. Store in a cool place. Fruit will be ready to eat in a month, but definitely improves with age.

Makes about 4 quarts.

Note More fruit can be added at any time. Toss each 2 cups fruit in ⅔ cup each white and firmly packed brown sugar and add enough brandy to cover.

Quick and easy sauces can be made out of many ingredients already in your cupboard. Experiment with your favorite liqueurs and confections, and perfect your own creations.

QUICK AND EASY SAUCES

A lack of time is no excuse for a lack of topping. The following quick and easy recipes will simplify your life and dazzle your guests.

APRICOT-ORANGE TOPPING

The quality of the apricot preserves will be reflected in the quality of the topping.

  2 tablespoons unsalted butter
  ½ cup apricot preserves
  ¼ cup orange juice
  ¼ teaspoon ground allspice

In a small saucepan over low heat melt butter. Add preserves and stir until melted. Stir in orange juice and allspice. Serve warm.

Makes about ¾ cup.

CHERRY SAUCE

George Washington himself would have loved this sauce.

  1 can (1 lb) pitted cherries
  ⅔ cup sugar
  2 tablespoons cornstarch
  ¼ teaspoon almond extract

Drain liquid from cherries into a small, heavy-bottomed saucepan. Add sugar and cornstarch and bring to a boil over medium heat. Reduce heat and simmer for 3 to 5 minutes. Add cherries and almond extract and cook for 1 minute more. Sauce may be served hot or cold.

Makes about 2 cups.

Cherry-Almond Sauce When sauce is cooked remove from heat and add ½ cup chopped, toasted almonds.

Black Forest Cherry Sauce When sauce is cooked remove from heat and stir in 1 tablespoon kirsch.

CARAMEL SAUCE

This sauce is a "quick fix" for caramel lovers.

½ pound caramel candies
1 cup whipping cream

Combine candies and cream in top of double boiler. Cook over hot water, stirring frequently, until candy is melted and well blended with cream.

Makes 1⅓ cups.

QUICK MARSHMALLOW TOPPING

Keep a jar of marshmallow cream on hand and you'll always be prepared for unexpected guests.

1 jar (7 oz) marshmallow cream
3 to 5 tablespoons water

In a small saucepan over moderate heat, melt marshmallow cream. Stir in 3 tablespoons of the water. For a thinner sauce add remaining water.

Makes 1 cup.

Spiked Marshmallow Topping Substitute 2 tablespoons liqueur, such as crème de menthe, Grand Marnier, or Tia Maria, for 2 tablespoons of the water.

Chocolate-Peppermint Topping Add 3 ounces chopped peppermint patties to marshmallow topping.

Marshmallow Fruit Topping Add ½ cup puréed fruit, such as peaches or apricots, with the marshmallow.

Spiced Marshmallow Topping Add ¼ teaspoon *each* ground nutmeg, ground ginger, and ground allspice with the marshmallow.

JAM SAUCE

Turn your favorite jam into an ice cream topping in no time.

1 cup jam
2 teaspoons cornstarch
⅔ cup cold water
2 teaspoons lemon juice

In a small, heavy-bottomed saucepan, heat jam over low heat until it melts. Mix cornstarch and the water, stir into jam, and bring to a boil. Lower heat and simmer about 2 minutes. Remove from heat and stir in lemon juice. Serve warm.

Makes about 1 cup.

QUICK CHOCOLATE SAUCE

This delicious one-step sauce is made entirely in a blender.

12 ounces chocolate chips
¼ cup hot water
1 tablespoon instant espresso powder

Place chocolate chips, hot water, and espresso powder in blender. Blend at medium speed until chocolate melts and sauce is smooth.

Makes about 1¼ cups.

YOGURT FRUIT SAUCE

Berries and soft fruits such as peaches or nectarines work best for this sauce.

2 cups chopped fresh fruit
3 tablespoons honey
⅓ cup plain yogurt

Mix fruit and honey; let stand about 1 hour. Combine with yogurt and chill.

Makes about 2 cups.

Yogurt Fruit Sauce Supreme Add 2 tablespoons brandy or orange-flavored liqueur with the yogurt.

Tips

THE SIMPLEST SAUCES

Crushed Fruit Fresh crushed fruit sauces are perhaps the easiest sauces to make. They are simple mixtures of fruit and sugar. (Although ripe fruit is extremely flavorful, most fruits benefit from a little sugar.) Berries, peaches, nectarines, and ripe pears are excellent fruits to use in these sauces. A good rule of thumb is to use ½ cup sugar for every 2 cups cut-up fruit. Purée the fruit in a food processor or blender or, if it is soft enough, mash it with a fork. Stir in the sugar. Allow the mixture to stand for an hour before serving. The sugar will cause the fruit to release its juices, enhancing its flavor.

Frozen Fruit Most frozen fruits can be used to make a quick and easy topping for ice cream. Serve the fruit when it has thawed slightly in its own syrup. The syrup will supply the needed sweetening. Keep your favorite frozen fruits on hand, and you'll always be ready to make a sauce in seconds.

*Thirst-quencher or dessert?
Either way, the fizz of ginger ale
combined with sweet-tart
Strawberry Ice Cream makes the
Strawberry Blondie a favorite.*

ICE CREAM SODAS

During the heyday of the soda fountain, the skill of soda jerks was often measured by the quality of their ice cream sodas. One sign of a great soda was that its scoop of ice cream hung on the edge of the glass, rather than sitting on the bottom. If the soda jerk's technique was finely honed, the ice cream lightly touched the soda water, melting at the point of contact and flavoring the drink.

An ice cream soda is composed of three basic parts: the flavoring; charged water, such as seltzer water or club soda; and ice cream. A swirl of whipped cream is often added to "finish it off."

COCONUT-GINGER ICE CREAM SODA

This tropical soda is sure to delight ginger lovers. The ginger has to steep in water for at least 8 hours, so start a day ahead.

Ginger Syrup

> 5 ounces fresh ginger, peeled and cut into quarter-sized pieces
> 2 cups water
> 1 cup sugar

Coconut Ice Cream

> 1 recipe French Vanilla Ice Cream Base II (see page 13)
> 1 package (7 oz) sweetened shredded coconut

1. If possible, make ice cream ahead and let it "ripen" in the freezer for several hours. Remove ice cream from freezer 10 to 15 minutes before assembling sodas.

2. To assemble: Follow directions for Making the Perfect Ice Cream Soda (at right).

Ginger Syrup

1. In a food processor fitted with a steel blade or in a blender in small batches, process ginger until it becomes pulpy.

2. In a small saucepan boil ginger in the water about 5 minutes. Set aside and let steep at room temperature for at least 8 hours.

3. Strain through a fine sieve into a clean saucepan, pressing hard to extract all the liquid. Add sugar and boil over medium-high heat until the mixture is slightly reduced (about 5 minutes). Refrigerate.

Makes about 1½ cups.

Coconut Ice Cream

1. Prepare French Vanilla Ice Cream Base II, adding coconut to milk and cream before you start to cook them.

2. Strain into a clean bowl (straining out the coconut) and cool thoroughly.

3. Transfer to an ice cream machine and freeze according to manufacturer's instructions.

Makes about 1 quart.

SODAS OF DISTINCTION

A number of sodas have earned permanent places in the ice cream hall of fame. These old favorites have been the pride of many a soda jerk.

Black and White made with chocolate syrup and vanilla (or French vanilla) ice cream.

Brown Cow made with root beer and vanilla ice cream.

Black Cow made with cola and vanilla ice cream.

Strawberry Blondie made with ginger ale, or Ginger Syrup (at left) and seltzer, and strawberry ice cream.

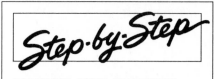

MAKING THE PERFECT ICE CREAM SODA

1. *Choose a suitably large glass. Put in about 2 tablespoons flavored syrup. (Use more or less, to taste.)*

2. *Fill the glass with charged water to within 2 inches of the rim. Mix well.*

3. *Position a scoop of ice cream on the edge of the glass, balanced so that its bottom touches the surface of the soda. If you wish, add a swirl of whipped cream. Serve with a long-handled spoon and a straw.*

MILKSHAKES, MALTEDS, FRAPPES, AND FLOATS

The ice cream soda may have given the soda fountain its name, but it was far from the only drink on the menu. Sodas have always shared the limelight with thick milkshakes, richly flavorful malteds, icy frappes, and simple but appealing floats. All of these popular drinks can be made at home with no special equipment.

MILKSHAKES

What you mean by "milkshake" depends on where you live or where you grew up. In some parts of the country a milkshake is just that, flavored milk shaken to a thick and foamy consistency. If ice cream is added, the milkshake becomes a frosted, a velvet, or a frappe. In other parts of the country, a milkshake is made with ice cream, and a frappe is a frozen slush, the definition most widely accepted and the one used here (see below).

The traditional soda fountain has a special machine for blending milkshakes, but you can make excellent milkshakes at home in an electric blender. There are only two basic rules. First, it is essential to use cold milk. Warm milk would melt the ice cream and thin the mixture. Second, don't overmix. Overmixing also makes a milkshake thin. Additions such as ripe, mashed bananas, berries, or flavored syrups add extra flavor, so be creative.

To make a milkshake, place ice cream, flavoring, and milk in a blender and mix. Relative quantities are a matter of taste. A simple rule of thumb is two large scoops of ice cream to one cup of milk, with flavoring added to taste.

ISLAND MILKSHAKE

This rum-laced treat is the next-best thing to an island getaway.

1 cup cold milk per serving

Banana-Rum Ice Cream

1 recipe French Vanilla Ice Cream Base II (see page 13)
3 large black-ripe bananas
½ cup sour cream
½ cup dark rum (see Note)

Pineapple Syrup

5 cups cubed fresh pineapple (1 medium-sized pineapple)
½ cup sugar

1. If possible, make ice cream ahead and let it "ripen" in the freezer for several hours. Remove ice cream from freezer 10 to 15 minutes before assembling milkshake.

2. To assemble: For each milkshake place 2 scoops ice cream and 1 cup milk in blender, add syrup to taste, and mix.

Banana-Rum Ice Cream

1. Prepare French Vanilla Ice Cream Base II. Strain into a clean bowl.

2. Mash bananas to make purée (3 bananas make about 1½ cups purée). Add bananas, sour cream, and rum to base. Cool thoroughly.

3. Transfer to an ice cream machine and freeze according to manufacturer's instructions.

Makes about 1 quart.

Pineapple Syrup

1. In a food processor fitted with a steel blade, purée pineapple. In a 2-quart saucepan combine purée with sugar. Bring to a boil over medium heat, stirring and washing down sides of pan with a pastry brush dipped in cold water. When sugar is dissolved, simmer mixture 10 minutes without stirring.

2. Remove from heat, cool to lukewarm, and strain through a fine sieve into a jar, pressing hard to extract all the liquid. Chill before using.

Makes 2½ cups.

Note The addition of rum slows down the freezing process slightly. Do not add any more rum or the mixture will not freeze properly.

MALTEDS

A malted is simply a milkshake to which malted milk powder has been added before blending. The inspiration for malt shops across the country, the malted has captured the taste buds of generations. The amount of malted milk powder depends on personal taste; any amount—from a single teaspoon to several tablespoons—is fine.

CHOCOLATE MALTED

Here is the best loved malted of all. The richness of the chocolate blends smoothly with the taste of malted milk powder. For some reason, fruit flavors do not taste right in malteds.

2 large scoops French Vanilla Ice Cream (see page 22)
1 cup milk
1 to 2 tablespoons malted milk powder
¼ cup Sweet Chocolate Syrup (see page 27) or Bittersweet Chocolate Syrup (see page 26)

Combine all ingredients and mix well in a blender.

Serves 1.

FRAPPES

Translated from the French, *frappe* literally means *chilled* or *iced*. In most places a frappe is a frozen slush mixture, made without dairy products. A simple sugar syrup is mixed with fruits or flavoring and partially frozen, then processed in a blender or food processor to the desired consistency. In some parts of the United States a milkshake made with ice cream is called a frappe, and in still other areas a frappe is carbonated water mixed with ice cream.

APRICOT FRAPPE

This light dessert is delicate in both color and flavor.

    2 cups apricots, peeled,
       stoned, and chopped
    1 cup sugar
    1½ cups water

1. In a small bowl lightly mash apricots.

2. In a small saucepan stir together sugar and the water. Cook over medium heat until sugar dissolves (3 to 5 minutes). Remove from heat. Add apricots and let cool.

3. Freeze until mixture is firm. Process in blender or food processor until slushy. Serve immediately.

Serves 4.

FLOATS

Ice cream floats are so easy to make, small children can make their own. Ice cream or sherbet and fruit juice or a carbonated soft drink are the only ingredients. Place a small amount of fruit juice or carbonated soft drink in the bottom of a large glass, then add 1 large scoop of ice cream or sherbet, mashing with a spoon to form a thick liquid. Add a second scoop of ice cream or sherbet. Fill the glass with more of the juice or soft drink.

Purple Cow To make this old favorite, combine vanilla ice cream and grape juice.

Cherry-Cola Float Combine cherry ice cream and cola.

A thick chocolate milkshake made in your own kitchen will bring back memories of your favorite soda fountain. Home-style soda jerks always leave their customers begging for more.

The rich golden colors of bourbon and toasted pecans make the Bourbon-Pecan Sundae as visually appealing as it is delicious.

SUNDAES

A sundae is the most free-form soda fountain creation, limited only by the scope of the imagination and the size of the dish. It can take the form of a single scoop of ice cream or a mountain of different flavors.

Since there are no hard and fast rules of sundae making, whatever appeals to you is acceptable: one scoop of ice cream or many, drizzled with a single sauce and topped with a delicate cloud of whipped cream or overflowing with a hodgepodge of nuts, syrups, toppings, fresh fruits, crushed candies, crumbled cookies, and whipped cream.

There are, however, a few guidelines to keep in mind. For greater visual appeal, alternate scoops of ice cream of contrasting colors, such as chocolate and vanilla, and crown ice creams with toppings of contrasting colors. For instance, put creamy white marshmallow topping on chocolate ice cream and dark, rich chocolate sauce on vanilla ice cream.

Consider using contrasting ice cream flavors, also. Try to match flavors that complement each other, not compete for attention.

BOURBON-PECAN SUNDAE WITH COFFEE ICE CREAM

Only a high-quality bourbon will do justice to this luscious sauce, which is a perfect foil for the rich coffee flavor of the ice cream.

- *1 recipe Coffee Ice Cream (see page 22)*
- *¼ cup toasted pecans, finely chopped (see Rocky Road Ice Cream, Note, page 22)*

Bourbon-Pecan Sauce

- *3 tablespoons unsalted butter*
- *¾ cup chopped pecans*
- *¾ cup maple syrup*
- *½ cup sugar*
- *⅓ cup whipping cream*
- *2 tablespoons bourbon*

1. If possible, make Coffee Ice Cream ahead and allow it to "ripen" for several hours in the freezer. Remove ice cream from freezer when you set Bourbon-Pecan Sauce aside to cool. Assemble sundaes within 10 to 15 minutes.

2. To assemble: For each sundae place 2 scoops ice cream in a chilled dessert bowl. Drizzle 2 tablespoons sauce over each scoop. Sprinkle chopped nuts on top.

Serves 4.

Bourbon-Pecan Sauce

1. In a small skillet melt butter and sauté pecans until they turn golden brown. Set aside.

2. In a small saucepan over medium heat, combine maple syrup, sugar, and cream. Cook until sugar is melted and mixture is smooth (about 5 minutes). Add bourbon and sautéed pecans. Cool slightly before using.

Makes about 2 cups.

CHOCOLATE-PEPPERMINT SUNDAE

The cool, nippy taste of peppermint sauce is a perfect complement to dark chocolate ice cream. If you want a more elaborate sundae, finish it off with a mound of unsweetened whipped cream and a decorative garnish, such as shaved chocolate or crushed peppermint candies.

Dark Chocolate Ice Cream

- *1 recipe French Vanilla Ice Cream Base I (see page 13)*
- *5 ounces semisweet chocolate*
- *3 ounces unsweetened chocolate*

Peppermint Sauce

- *½ pound hard peppermint candies, crushed*
- *1 cup water*
- *½ cup sugar*

1. If possible, make Dark Chocolate Ice Cream ahead and allow it to "ripen" for several hours in the freezer. Remove ice cream from freezer when you set Peppermint Sauce aside to cool (or 10 to 15 minutes before serving if sauce is made ahead).

2. To assemble: For each serving place 2 scoops ice cream in a chilled dessert bowl. Drizzle 2 tablespoons sauce over each scoop.

Serves 4.

Dark Chocolate Ice Cream

1. Melt chocolates together in a double boiler. Meanwhile, prepare French Vanilla Ice Cream Base I and strain into a clean bowl.

2. Add ½ cup of warm ice cream base to melted chocolate, whisking constantly to keep chocolate smooth. Return mixture to ice cream base, mix well, and let cool.

3. Transfer to an ice cream machine and freeze according to manufacturer's instructions.

Makes about 1 quart.

Peppermint Sauce In a small, heavy-bottomed saucepan, heat candies and the water over medium heat, stirring occasionally, until candies begin to melt. Boil for a few minutes, then add sugar and stir until it dissolves. Cool.

Makes 2 cups.

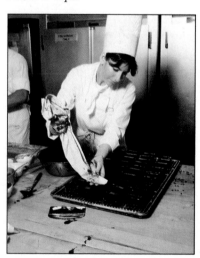

VANILLA-TOP BANANA SPLIT

Adding a banana to a sundae transforms it into a royale or banana split. The traditional banana split has three ice cream flavors, three sauces, a banana, whipped cream, nuts, and maraschino cherries. This recipe makes a lavish and well balanced banana split; you can easily substitute other ice creams and sauces. Start at least a day ahead if you are going to make all your own ice creams. Of course, one or more ice creams can be storebought.

1 recipe Vanilla Sauce
  (see page 30)
3 tablespoons cranberry sauce
¼ cup toasted nuts, any kind, chopped (see Rocky Road Ice Cream, Note, page 22)
8 to 10 bananas
2 to 2½ cups whipping cream
24 to 30 maraschino cherries

Fresh Berry Ice Cream

2 pints fresh berries, any kind
¼ cup sugar, or to taste
1 recipe French Vanilla Ice Cream Base II (see page 13)
2 teaspoons lemon juice (optional)

White Chocolate Ice Cream

1 pound white chocolate
3 cups whipping cream
1 cup milk
1 vanilla bean, split lengthwise
10 large egg yolks

Mocha Ice Cream

1 recipe Chocolate Ice Cream (see page 22)
1 tablespoon instant espresso powder

1. If possible, make ice creams ahead and allow them to "ripen" for several hours in the freezer. Remove ice cream from freezer 10 to 15 minutes before assembling banana splits.

2. Prepare Vanilla Sauce. While still warm, divide into thirds. Stir cranberry sauce into one third. Let second third cool, then stir in chopped nuts. Leave remaining third plain.

3. For each banana split, peel banana and split lengthwise. Lay halves in bottom of long dessert dish. Place one scoop of each ice cream in a row on top. Drizzle plain Vanilla Sauce on Fresh Berry Ice Cream, cranberry vanilla sauce on White Chocolate Ice Cream, and vanilla nut sauce on Mocha Ice Cream. Whip the cream to soft peaks. Using a pastry bag with a number 7 star tip, top each scoop with a swirl of cream. Place a cherry atop each swirl.

Serves 8 to 10.

Fresh Berry Ice Cream

1. In a large bowl mash berries with sugar. Let stand about 1 hour.

2. Meanwhile, prepare French Vanilla Ice Cream Base II. Strain into a clean bowl and cool thoroughly.

3. If berries are not very flavorful, stir in lemon juice to heighten taste. Purée in a food processor or blender, then strain. Add purée to ice cream base. Transfer to an ice cream machine and freeze according to manufacturer's instructions.

Makes about 1 quart.

White Chocolate Ice Cream

1. Coarsely chop white chocolate.

2. In a heavy-bottomed 2-quart saucepan, combine chocolate, cream, and milk. Scrape seeds from vanilla bean into mixture, then add pod. Cook over low heat, stirring occasionally, until chocolate is melted.

3. In a medium bowl beat egg yolks until they are light and lemon colored. Remove vanilla pod from chocolate mixture and discard. Whisk 1 cup of chocolate mixture into egg yolks, then pour egg mixture back into chocolate, whisking constantly to keep eggs from cooking. Strain into a clean bowl and cool.

4. Transfer to an ice cream machine and freeze according to manufacturer's instructions.

Makes about 1 quart.

Mocha Ice Cream Prepare Chocolate Ice Cream, stirring espresso powder into warm ice cream base before adding base to chocolate.

Makes about 1 quart.

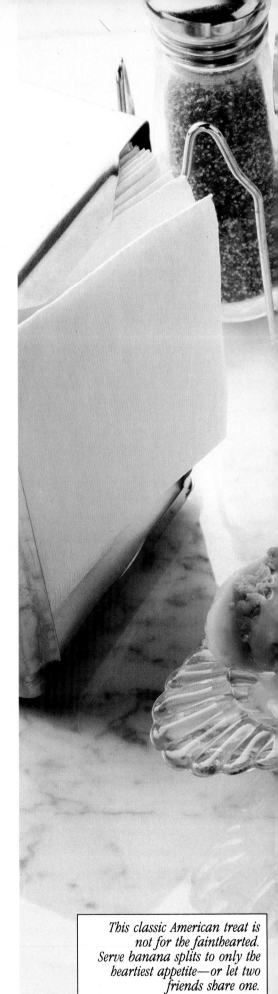

This classic American treat is not for the fainthearted. Serve banana splits to only the heartiest appetite—or let two friends share one.

PARFAITS AND COUPES

There is often confusion about the term *parfait*. The American parfait, as served at the soda fountain, is a layered sundae in a tall, slender glass. It is simple to make: Just alternate layers of ice cream and topping. Another poorly understood soda fountain term is *coupe*. A coupe is ice cream served with fruit topping.

BUTTER PECAN–HOT FUDGE PARFAIT

This is an elegant yet simple dessert. The Hot Fudge Sauce is the old-fashioned type that hardens and slides down the ice cream.

Butter Pecan Ice Cream

1 recipe French Vanilla Ice Cream Base II (see page 13), without sugar

¾ cup firmly packed light brown sugar

3 tablespoons unsalted butter, melted

1 cup chopped, toasted pecans (see Rocky Road Ice Cream, Note, page 22)

Hot Fudge Sauce

6 tablespoons unsalted butter

½ cup water

4 ounces unsweetened chocolate

1 cup sugar

3 tablespoons light corn syrup

⅛ teaspoon salt

2 teaspoons vanilla extract

1. Remove ice cream from the freezer when you begin making the sauce, so ice cream will have time to soften slightly before serving.

2. To assemble: For each parfait, place 1 scoop ice cream in a tall glass. Top with 2 tablespoons sauce. Alternate as many layers of ice cream and sauce as desired or as many as the glass will hold.

Serves 4.

Butter Pecan Ice Cream

1. Prepare French Vanilla Ice Cream Base II using brown sugar and butter instead of sugar. Strain into a clean bowl and cool thoroughly.

2. Transfer to an ice cream machine and begin to freeze according to manufacturer's instructions. Midway through freezing process, add pecans. Complete freezing.

Makes about 1 quart.

Hot Fudge Sauce

1. In a heavy-bottomed 1-quart saucepan, melt butter in the water over medium heat. Bring to a boil, stirring constantly.

2. Add chocolate, stirring occasionally until it melts. (Chocolate may lump; it will smooth out later.)

3. Add sugar, corn syrup, and salt. Boil 5 minutes. Remove from heat and add vanilla. Serve hot.

Makes about 2 cups.

FRESH CHERRY COUPE

If you make the ice cream and sauce in advance, you can put this delicious dessert together in seconds.

1 recipe French Vanilla Ice Cream (see page 22)

Fresh Cherry Sauce

1 pound Bing or Royal Ann cherries, pitted

½ cup sugar

¼ cup plus 2 tablespoons cold water

1 teaspoon cornstarch

2 teaspoons lemon juice

1. If possible, make ice cream ahead and let it "ripen" for several hours in the freezer. Remove ice cream from freezer 10 to 15 minutes before assembling coupes.

2. To assemble: Place a scoop of ice cream in a chilled dessert dish. Top with sauce.

Serves 8.

Fresh Cherry Sauce

1. In a small heavy-bottomed saucepan, combine cherries, sugar, and ¼ cup of the water. Cook over medium heat until cherries start giving off their juices and sugar is dissolved. Simmer a few minutes longer.

2. Dissolve cornstarch in remaining water, add to cherry mixture, and simmer until sauce thickens slightly (a few minutes). Transfer to a bowl, add lemon juice, and let cool. Chill before using.

Makes about 1½ cups.

DOUBLE-STRAWBERRY COUPE

Try this intensely flavorful combination when strawberries are at their peak of ripeness.

1 recipe Strawberry Ice Cream (see page 22)

Strawberry Sauce

2 cups strawberries, chopped

½ cup sugar

2 to 4 tablespoons water (optional)

1. If possible, make the ice cream ahead and let it "ripen" in the freezer for several hours. If sauce is to be served hot, remove ice cream from freezer when you begin cooking sauce. Otherwise, take ice cream out 10 to 15 minutes before serving.

2. To assemble: For each coupe place a scoop of ice cream in a chilled dessert dish. Top with sauce.

Serves 8.

Strawberry Sauce

In a small bowl combine strawberries and sugar; let stand about 1 hour. In a small saucepan over medium heat, cook berry mixture about 5 minutes, mashing berries as they cook. Add the water 1 tablespoon at a time if berries are not very juicy. Serve hot or cold.

Makes about 2 cups.

Clear glass dishes show off the colors and textures of ice cream parfaits and coupes. Let your imagination run wild to create a favorite combination.

By the truckload or more conventionally served, ice cream Bonbons (see page 53) are always a hit. Keep some in your freezer for unexpected guests.

Special Treats

Frozen desserts and snacks always seem special. For adults, ice cream desserts, especially those laced with luscious liqueurs (see pages 46 to 48), are the perfect endings for company dinners or romantic evenings. Frozen drinks (see pages 48 to 49) are refreshing on lazy summer afternoons, bringing with them memories—or dreams— of vacations in exotic, tropical places. For children, frozen treats mean birthday parties, days at the beach, and the ice cream truck coming down the street at last. Ice cream has a way of adding sparkle to any occasion. What could be more fun to eat than birthday cake and ice cream? Well, how about ice cream Bonbons (see page 53) or an ice cream pizza (see page 60)?

The humble ice cream sandwich takes on new sophistication when made with chocolate madeleines and your favorite ice cream.

In a small saucepan over medium heat, combine pineapple with its juice, lemon juice, and cornstarch. Bring to a boil, then immediately remove from heat and let cool. Stir in crème de menthe. Scoop ice cream into 4 chilled dessert dishes and top with sauce.

Makes about 2 cups sauce, serves 4.

RUSTY NAIL PARFAIT

This is a true French parfait. Serve in tall, slender glasses.

> 1 large egg, plus 2 large yolks
> ¼ cup sugar
> 3 tablespoons water
> ¼ cup Scotch whisky
> 1 cup whipping cream
> 6 tablespoons Scotch whisky liqueur
> 4 almond macaroons
> ¼ cup slivered almonds, toasted (optional; see Rocky Road Ice Cream, Note, page 22)

1. In a bowl beat together egg and egg yolks until fluffy and lemon colored. Set aside.

2. In a small, heavy-bottomed saucepan, heat sugar and the water to the soft-ball stage (240° F on a candy thermometer). Pour sugar syrup slowly into egg mixture, beating constantly. Continue beating until mixture is cool to the touch. Stir in Scotch whisky.

3. Beat the cream until stiff. Fold into egg mixture. Into each parfait glass, pour 1½ tablespoons whisky liqueur, add a few tablespoons of parfait mixture, and top with a macaroon. Fill glasses with remaining parfait mixture.

4. Freeze until set (about 2 hours). Let stand at room temperature about 5 minutes before serving. Garnish with slivered almonds.

Serves 4.

TREATS FOR ADULTS

Everyone loves a festive dessert. Even when the day is especially hectic, you can serve beautiful desserts that will delight company and give you a much-deserved treat. The following satisfyingly "adult" desserts can all be made in minutes as long as you have a container of ice cream in the freezer.

MINT JULEP SUNDAE

Pineapple and mint make an especially refreshing combination.

> 1 can (1 lb) crushed pineapple
> 1 tablespoon lemon juice
> 2 teaspoons cornstarch
> ¼ cup crème de menthe
> 1 recipe Bourbon Ice Cream (see page 93) or French Vanilla Ice Cream (see page 22)

CHOCOLATE MADELEINE ICE CREAM SANDWICHES

These are sophisticated, thoroughly adult ice cream sandwiches. You will need madeleine pans to make the cookies. This batter is thicker than the traditional madeleine batter, resulting in a denser cookie, capable of holding the ice cream in a sandwich.

> 2 large eggs, separated
> ½ cup sugar
> ½ cup Dutch-process cocoa
> ½ cup flour, sifted
> 1 teaspoon baking powder
> Pinch of salt
> 4 tablespoons unsalted butter, softened
> 1 teaspoon vanilla extract
> 1 pint ice cream, any flavor

1. Preheat oven to 425° F. Butter 2 madeleine pans (for 24 cookies). In a medium bowl beat together egg yolks and sugar until well mixed. Whisk in cocoa. In another bowl combine flour, baking powder, and salt. Fold flour mixture into yolk mixture, then incorporate butter and vanilla.

2. Whisk egg whites until they form stiff peaks. Fold into batter. Fill each mold two thirds full. Bake until madeleines are firm to the touch (10 to 15 minutes). Remove from pan and let cool on racks.

3. Using an oval ice cream scoop, place 1 scoop ice cream on flat side of a cooled madeleine. Place another madeleine, flat side down, on top. Press together gently. Repeat with remaining madeleines. Wrap individual sandwiches tightly and freeze.

Makes 12 sandwiches.

Special Feature

ICE CREAM CORDIALS

Quick and easy does not have to mean inelegant. Ice Cream Cordials are no more than ice cream topped with liqueur and sometimes a garnish, but they are the perfect end to a special dinner. You can either soften the ice cream and fold in the liqueur (about 2 tablespoons of liqueur per pint of ice cream) or drizzle the liqueur over scoops of ice cream. Try the following guaranteed-to-sparkle combinations or create your own.

French Vanilla Ice Cream
(see page 22)
Cranberry-flavored liqueur
Coffee-flavored liqueur and a light sprinkling of freshly ground coffee
Pear-flavored liqueur and chocolate shavings

Coffee Ice Cream
(see page 22)
Cognac and toasted almonds
Scotch whisky liqueur

Chocolate Ice Cream
(see page 22)
Orange-flavored liqueur and chopped candied orange peel
Dark rum and toasted coconut

Strawberry Ice Cream
(see page 22)
Crème de cassis
Crème de framboise

Fresh Peach Ice Cream (see Fresh Fruit Ice Cream, page 25)
Peach or apricot brandy
Amaretto and crushed *amaretti* (Italian macaroons)

Maple-Walnut Ice Cream
(see page 23)
Crème de cacao and a sprinkling of cocoa powder
Coffee-flavored liqueur

Butter Pecan Ice Cream
(see page 42)
Irish whiskey liqueur and toasted pecans
Cognac

Peanut Butter Ice Cream
(see page 25)
Calvados or applejack
Chocolate-orange liqueur and chocolate shavings

SPLIT BANANAS

This is an adult version of a classic childhood favorite.

  1 cup unsalted butter
  1 cup firmly packed light
    brown sugar
  4 large bananas, peeled
    and sliced into rounds
  4 tablespoons lemon juice
  4 teaspoons granulated sugar
  4 tablespoons orange-
    flavored liqueur
  2 tablespoon kirsch or banana
    or other fruit-flavored liqueur
  1 cup whipping cream
  1 recipe French Vanilla
    Ice Cream (see page 22)
  1 cup toasted macadamia nuts,
    chopped (see Rocky Road
    Ice Cream, Note, page 22)

1. In a medium saucepan melt butter over moderate heat. Add brown sugar and stir until melted. Add banana slices and stir to coat. Blend in lemon juice, granulated sugar, liqueur, and kirsch. Simmer 2 minutes.

2. Whip the cream to soft peaks. Divide ice cream into 4 chilled dessert dishes. Spoon hot sauce over ice cream. Top with whipped cream and chopped nuts.

Serves 4.

FROZEN DRINKS

Frozen drinks are delightful refreshers that can be served year round. Freezing adds a touch of class to ordinary drinks and puts new sparkle into many an old favorite. It changes a simple wine spritzer into a surprising, refreshing slush (right). Blended with Rum-Raisin Ice Cream (see page 25), your favorite Cognac is transformed into a Cognac Cocktail (right), a distinctly adult cooler. Since alcohol keeps any mixture it's in from freezing rock hard, your drinks will have an icy, slushy texture. Serve them in crystal glasses with silver spoons at special parties or sip them from tumblers on hot days by the pool.

COGNAC COCKTAIL

Especially elegant served in large wine glasses.

  4 scoops Rum-Raisin Ice Cream
    (see page 25)
  6 ounces Cognac
    Ground cinnamon, to taste
    (optional)

In a blender or food processor, blend ice cream and Cognac until smooth. Pour into large wine glasses. Sprinkle with cinnamon, if desired.

Serves 4.

FROZEN GIN AND TONIC

Instead of drinks on the patio on those hot days, try serving this frozen delight in tall glasses with long-handled silver spoons.

    Zest of 2 limes, finely chopped
  ½ cup sugar
  ¼ cup lime juice
  ⅓ cup gin
  1 large bottle (28 oz)
    tonic water

1. In a small bowl crush together lime zest and sugar until well combined. Let stand about 30 minutes.

2. Transfer sugar and lime zest mixture to a large container. Stir in lime juice and gin, then slowly pour in tonic water. Chill. When cold, transfer to an ice cream machine and freeze according to manufacturer's instructions.

Makes about 1 quart.

WHITE WINE FROST

The type of wine you choose will determine how sweet this drink is.

  2 cups sweet or dry white wine
  ¼ cup sugar
  1 teaspoon lemon juice

Combine all ingredients. Transfer to an ice cream machine and freeze according to manufacturer's directions. Serve in glasses or dessert bowls with spoons.

Serves 4.

FROZEN MARGARITAS

Use freshly squeezed lime juice for the best taste.

  1 ounce lime juice
  1 ounce orange-flavored liqueur
  1½ ounces white tequila
  ¾ cup cracked ice

Combine all ingredients in a blender. Purée to slushy consistency. Serve immediately.

Serves 1.

FROZEN WINE SPRITZER

This is a wonderful variation on a popular summer refresher.

  1 cup dry red wine
  1¼ cups water
  1 cup sugar
  ¼ cup lemon juice
    Zest of 3 lemons,
    finely chopped
  1 bottle (16 oz) club soda,
    chilled

1. In a medium saucepan combine wine, 1 cup of the water, and sugar. Cook over low heat, stirring and washing down sides of pan with a brush dipped in cold water, until sugar is dissolved. Cook over moderate heat for 5 minutes without stirring. Remove from heat and let cool.

2. Stir in the remaining water, lemon juice, and lemon zest. Transfer to an ice cream machine and freeze according to manufacturer's instructions.

3. When frozen, scoop into large, chilled goblets, then fill goblets with chilled club soda.

Serves 4.

FROZEN WINE COOLER

This is a really quick and easy treat.

    Bottled wine cooler, as
    much as you want

Freeze in an ice cream machine according to manufacturer's instructions.

GLORIA'S GLORIOUS DISASTER

This cool treat is not for the faint of heart.

¾ cup bourbon
¼ cup grenadine
¼ cup lemon juice
2 cups shaved ice

Combine bourbon, grenadine, and lemon juice. Divide ice among 4 glasses and fill with bourbon mixture.

Serves 4.

KENTUCKY DERBY SLUSH

You don't have to wait for race day to enjoy this.

2 tablespoons chopped mint leaves
1 tablespoon sugar
2 ounces bourbon
3 cups crushed ice

Combine all ingredients in a blender. Purée until mixture is smooth. Pour into frosty highball glasses and serve immediately.

Serves 2.

Turn your next party into a fiesta. Frozen Margaritas make ideal party fare for grown-ups in any country.

MAKE YOUR OWN EDIBLE DISHES

With just a little effort, you can make edible containers for your favorite ice cream. The distinctive shapes and wonderful, butter-rich flavors of *pizzelles* (right) and *tuiles* (opposite page) will impress both family and guests.

Tuile   *Remove a hot tuile from the baking sheet with a spatula and drape it over a rolling pin. Let it cool enough to hold its shape, then transfer it to a wire rack.*

Cylinder   *As you remove each hot tuile from the baking sheet, roll it into a cylinder. Overlap the edges slightly and pinch them together. When ready to serve, use a pastry bag to fill each cylinder with ice cream.*

Cup   *Remove a hot tuile from the baking sheet with a spatula and drape it loosely over an inverted custard cup to cool. Do not shape it with your fingers.*

Tulip   *Drape a hot tuile over an inverted custard cup (as above). While still hot, gently press it down around the sides of the cup. This makes the rim of the cookie cup wavy rather than round.*

Taco shell   *Lift a hot pizzelle from the iron (as in Make Your Own Ice Cream Cones, page 51, step 1) and drape it over a suspended broom handle or dowel. Let it cool enough to hold its shape, then transfer it to a wire rack.*

PERFECT PARTNERS

Cookies are naturals with ice cream.

PIZZELLES

These versatile cookies can be formed into ice cream cones, cylinders, cups, or even taco-like shells (see photographs at left and on page 51).

    1 cup unsalted butter
    6 eggs
 1½ cups sugar
    2 tablespoons vanilla extract
 3½ cups flour
    4 teaspoons baking powder

1. Melt butter over low heat; let cool. Beat eggs with an electric mixer. While beating, add sugar in a steady stream; continue beating until smooth. Add cooled butter and vanilla extract, then mix in flour and baking powder.

2. Bake in pizzelle iron (see page 9) according to manufacturer's instructions.

Makes about 50 pizzelles.

KOURABIEDES

This popular cookie of Greek origin is often served at holiday celebrations.

 1½ cups unsalted butter, at
        room temperature
    2 tablespoons confectioners'
        sugar
    1 large egg yolk
  ½ cup ground almonds
 3½ cups flour
        Confectioners' sugar,
        for dusting

1. Preheat oven to 275° F. Lightly grease baking sheet. In a medium bowl cream butter and 2 tablespoons sugar. Mix in egg yolk and then almonds. Gradually add flour to make a stiff dough.

2. Form balls of dough about 1 inch in diameter. Using your thumb, indent the center of each ball and shape it into a crescent.

3. Bake cookies 45 minutes. Cool to lukewarm, then generously dust with confectioners' sugar.

Makes 4 dozen cookies.

TUILES

These wonderful French cookies are named after the roof tiles in France. They can be molded over cups to make elegant little bowls for ice cream (see opposite page).

> 4 tablespoons unsalted butter, softened
> ½ cup sugar
> 2 large egg whites, lightly beaten
> 5 tablespoons flour
> ⅓ cup ground almonds
> ¼ teaspoon almond extract
> ½ teaspoon vanilla extract

1. Preheat oven to 425° F. Lightly grease baking sheet.

2. In a medium bowl beat together butter and sugar until fluffy. Blend in egg whites. Fold in flour, almonds, and almond and vanilla extracts.

3. Drop teaspoonfuls of batter 3 inches apart on greased baking sheet. With the back of a spoon, spread each mound into a 2½-inch-diameter circle. Bake until lightly browned around the edges (about 4 minutes). While cookies are still warm, drape them over a rolling pin and let cool (see opposite page).

Makes about 18 cookies.

BOMBAY DELIGHTS

These crispy curried cookies are meant for an adult's seasoned palate. Try them with Coconut Ice Cream (see page 35).

> 1 cup unsalted butter, at room temperature
> 2 cups firmly packed dark brown sugar
> 2 teaspoons vanilla extract
> 2 large eggs, beaten
> 1½ cups unsalted peanuts, chopped
> ¼ cup golden raisins, chopped
> 3 cups flour
> ½ teaspoon baking soda
> 1 teaspoon baking powder
> ½ teaspoon salt
> 1 tablespoon curry powder

1. In a large bowl cream butter with brown sugar. Add vanilla and eggs, then mix in peanuts and raisins.

2. In a medium bowl sift together flour, baking soda, baking powder, salt, and curry. Add flour mixture to butter mixture and combine well.

3. Form dough into 2 cylinders, each about 1½ inches in diameter. Wrap individually in waxed paper and freeze until firm.

4. Preheat oven to 350° F. While cookie dough is still frozen, cut each cylinder into ¼-inch-thick slices. Bake on ungreased baking sheets until lightly browned (12 to 15 minutes). Let cool on sheets about 5 minutes, then remove to racks.

Makes about 4 dozen cookies.

SNAPPERS

These tasty little cookies can be made in a snap.

> ½ cup unsalted butter, at room temperature
> ¾ cup sugar
> 3 tablespoons molasses
> ½ teaspoon vanilla extract
> 1½ teaspoons ground ginger
> ½ teaspoon freshly grated nutmeg
> 1½ cups flour
> ¾ teaspoon baking soda
>   Pinch of salt
> ¼ teaspoon each ground cloves and ground cinnamon

1. Preheat oven to 350° F. In a medium bowl cream butter and ¼ cup of the sugar. Beat in molasses and vanilla. In a small bowl combine ginger, nutmeg, flour, baking soda, salt, cloves, and cinnamon. Stir into the butter mixture to form a dough.

2. Place dough on a baking sheet lined with plastic wrap; cover with plastic wrap. Roll out dough to 1 inch thick. Chill at least 30 minutes.

3. Pinch off balls of dough, about 2 teaspoonfuls each, or use a number 100 ice cream scoop to form balls. Roll balls in remaining sugar to coat. Place balls on parchment-lined baking sheets; flatten them slightly with a fork. Bake until lightly browned (12 to 15 minutes). Cool on racks.

Makes about 3 dozen cookies.

Special Feature

MAKE YOUR OWN ICE CREAM CONES

Hot *pizzelles* are easily shaped into sturdy, crisp cones.

1. Lift the edge of the hot pizzelle with a knife and carefully peel it from the iron.

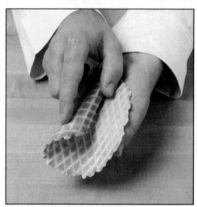

2. Roll one side toward the center to begin forming a cone.

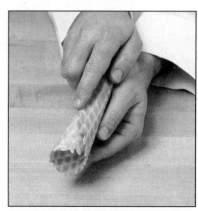

3. Wrap the opposite side around to complete the cone shape. Pinch the overlapping edges together.

Waffles aren't just for breakfast anymore. Enjoy Chocolate Waffles and ice cream any time of day.

CHOCOLATE WAFFLES

With or without nuts, these chocolaty waffles make a wonderful base for ice cream and sauces.

  1½ cups flour
  ¼ cup cocoa powder
  1 teaspoon baking powder
  1 teaspoon baking soda
  ⅓ cup sugar
  2 cups buttermilk
  ½ cup vegetable oil or melted butter
  2 large eggs, separated
  1 teaspoon vanilla extract
    Pinch cream of tartar
  1 cup chopped pecans (optional)

1. Sift together flour, cocoa, baking powder, baking soda, and sugar. Make a well in center of sifted dry ingredients.

2. In a separate bowl, mix buttermilk, oil, egg yolks, and vanilla. Pour into the well and mix with dry ingredients.

3. Beat egg whites with cream of tartar until soft peaks form. Gradually fold into batter, one third at a time. Fold in pecans (if used).

4. Cook in waffle iron according to manufacturer's instructions.

Makes 4 large waffles.

TREATS FOR KIDS

Kids love frozen treats, served as a special dessert, party favors, or a simple afternoon snack. Ice cream is so easy to work with and so full of possibilities, it is an open invitation to artistic creativity. Besides experimenting with mixing and matching flavors and textures, take advantage of the ease with which ice cream can be shaped. With very little effort you can delight the younger set with jolly Ice Cream Clowns (see page 54), a smashing snowman centerpiece (see page 54), or an unforgettable ice cream pizza (see page 60).

FROZEN CHOCOLATE BANANAS

These are a favorite with kids any time of the year.

> 6 large, firm bananas
> 12 wooden ice cream sticks
> 12 ounces semisweet chocolate
> 2 tablespoons vegetable shortening
> Toppings, such as shredded coconut, chopped nuts, sprinkles, or granola (optional)

1. Peel bananas and halve them crosswise. Insert a stick into the cut end of each banana half and push it in half the length of the fruit. Freeze bananas until hard on a baking sheet lined with waxed paper. (Bananas must be frozen or chocolate will not adhere to them.)

2. In a small, heavy-bottomed saucepan over moderate heat, melt chocolate with shortening. Stir until smooth. Let cool slightly, for 2 to 3 minutes.

3. Remove prepared bananas from freezer. Dip each into chocolate mixture, turning to coat completely. Use a spatula to help cover bananas, if necessary. Roll chocolate-covered bananas in toppings (if desired). Replace on baking sheet.

4. Return to freezer. When chocolate and toppings are firm, wrap each chocolate banana tightly and store in freezer. Let thaw a few minutes before serving.

Makes 12 bananas.

Honey Bananas Cut bananas and insert sticks as directed in step 1. Before freezing, roll bananas in honey, then in chopped, salted peanuts. Freeze as directed in step 4.

PEANUT BUTTER PIE

This is an easy, sophisticated update of a longtime favorite.

> 1 pint French Vanilla Ice Cream (see page 22), softened slightly
> ½ cup chunky peanut butter, at room temperature
> ½ cup crushed unsalted peanuts
> 1 tablespoon vanilla extract
> 1 8-inch graham cracker crust, baked and cooled
> 1 cup whipping cream (optional)

In a large bowl combine ice cream, peanut butter, ¼ cup of the peanuts, and vanilla. Mix well, then pour into prepared crust. Sprinkle with remaining peanuts and freeze. Whip the cream (if used) and decorate pie before serving.

Serves 6 to 8.

BLACK AND WHITES

Ice cream and cake is always a favorite combination. These double-chocolate cupcakes have a scoop of vanilla ice cream hidden inside.

> 3 eggs
> 1 cup sugar
> ¼ cup unsalted butter
> 3 ounces white chocolate, chopped
> 1¼ cups flour
> 1 heaping teaspoon baking powder
> ¼ teaspoon salt
> 4 ounces semisweet chocolate, finely chopped
> 1 pint French Vanilla Ice Cream (see page 22)

1. Preheat oven to 350° F. In a heavy-bottomed 2-quart saucepan over very low heat, beat together eggs and sugar. Add butter and white chocolate. Stir just until butter and chocolate melt and mixture is smooth. It should be warm, not hot, to the touch.

2. In a medium bowl mix flour, baking powder, and salt. Add to white chocolate mixture and beat until blended. Drop in chopped semisweet chocolate and stir just until chocolate begins to melt and create a marbled effect. Do not overblend.

3. Spoon batter into cupcake pans lined with paper baking cups, filling each cup about three fourths full. Bake until tops spring back when lightly touched (about 20 minutes). Remove to wire racks to cool. Cupcakes will sink slightly as they cool.

4. When cupcakes are cool, cut top off each. With a melon baller remove a small scoop from the lower half of each. Fill each cupcake with a scoop of French Vanilla Ice Cream, replace top, wrap individually in freezer wrap, and freeze. Serve directly from freezer or thaw slightly before serving.

Makes 12 cupcakes.

BONBONS

Bonbons work well with any flavor ice cream. Peanut Butter Ice Cream (see page 25) is a favorite with both young and older children. To transform Bonbons into an adult confection, use Bourbon Ice Cream (see page 93).

> 1 pint ice cream, any flavor
> 12 ounces semisweet chocolate
> 2 tablespoons unsalted butter

1. Chill a baking sheet lined with waxed paper in the freezer for about 20 minutes. With a small ice cream scoop or large melon baller, scoop small balls of ice cream onto sheet. Return sheet with balls to freezer until balls are very firm.

2. In a small, heavy-bottomed saucepan, melt chocolate with butter, stirring until mixture is smooth. Let cool to almost room temperature.

3. Insert a fork into one ice cream ball at a time and dip ball into chocolate mixture, covering ball completely; return it to the baking sheet. Work quickly and return Bonbons to the freezer as soon as possible.

Makes 24 to 30 Bonbons.

KALEIDOSCOPE ICE CREAM

Nostalgic memories of childhood include the magic of looking through a kaleidoscope and seeing the lively spectrum of vibrant colors and patterns. The addition of colorful confections to your favorite ice cream will create the same feeling. Mixed-in tidbits instantly transform plain ice cream into a party treat for the younger set. Simply soften the desired amount of ice cream and fold in your kids' favorites. Some of the most common choices include candy-coated chocolates, chocolate-covered peanut butter cups (chopped), miniature chocolate chips, colored sprinkles, jimmies, gumdrops, miniature marshmallows, and granola. Almost any bite-sized treat will work. Break your children's favorite cookies into small pieces and mix them in. For Christmas fold in red and green candied cherries.

A fast way to soften ice cream is to place the container in the microwave oven for 10 to 20 seconds.

ICE CREAM CLOWNS

These are perfect for children's parties.

> 1 quart ice cream, any flavor
> 3 ounces semisweet chocolate
> 2 teaspoons vegetable shortening or unsalted butter
> 8 ice cream cones
> ⅓ cup sprinkles
> Green and red gumdrops

1. Freeze a baking sheet lined with waxed paper for at least 20 minutes. Scoop 8 large ice cream balls (to be used as clown heads) onto sheet and return to freezer until very firm.

2. In a small, heavy-bottomed saucepan, melt chocolate and shortening over moderate heat. Stir until smooth. Brush onto outside of ice cream cones. While chocolate is still warm, roll cones in sprinkles. Set aside.

3. Remove ice cream balls from freezer. Use gumdrops to form eyes and mouth of each clown head. Place a decorated cone upside down on each ball to form a hat. Serve immediately on chilled dessert plates with spoons.

Serves 8.

CHOCOLATE BIRD'S NESTS

This is one of the simplest confections to make.

> 8 ounces semisweet chocolate, chopped
> 1 cup canned chow mein noodles
> ½ cup chopped unsalted peanuts
> 2 cups light-colored ice cream, any flavor

1. Melt chocolate in a small, heavy-bottomed saucepan over low heat. Stir in noodles and peanuts. Let cool slightly.

2. Make 4 mounds of chocolate mixture on a sheet of waxed paper. With a spoon make an indentation in the middle of each mound to form a "nest." Cool; then refrigerate.

3. When firm, fill each nest with small scoops of ice cream formed with an oval scoop to look like eggs.

Serves 4.

SNOWMAN ON A SLEIGH

This whimsical creation can ride on any size candy canes. Made large, it is a delightful centerpiece (although one that must be eaten quickly); made small (use 2½-inch candy canes and about 1 cup of ice cream per serving), it is a memorable individual party dessert.

> 1 square of ice cream, any flavor
> 2 candy canes
> 2 balls of ice cream, any flavor, one larger than the other
> ½ to 1 cup chopped coconut
> 1 round chocolate sandwich cookie
> 3 miniature gumdrops
> 1 marshmallow
> 1 strip licorice

1. To form sleigh: To make squares of ice cream, soften desired amount of ice cream, form it into a block, and freeze it on a baking sheet until firm. Slice into squares.

2. On a baking sheet lined with waxed paper, position candy canes parallel to one another, curved ends up, and place square of ice cream on top to make a sleigh. Press down lightly on ice cream so it adheres to candy canes. Freeze until firm.

3. To form snowman: Shape ice cream balls for the snowman's body and head, taking into consideration size of sleigh. Roll balls in chopped coconut until well covered. Freeze on baking sheet until firm.

4. Place smaller ball of ice cream on top of larger one. Press down so balls adhere to each other. Scrape away some of the coconut where balls touch if they fail to stick together.

5. Place chocolate cookie on top of small ball of ice cream to form base of hat. Cut a thin slice from center of gumdrop. Place slice on top of cookie and press marshmallow on top to form body of hat. Use remaining gumdrops to form eyes and strip of licorice for mouth. Set snowman on sleigh. Serve immediately or freeze until ready to serve.

Makes 1 snowman.

It's like having Frosty the
Snowman himself come to your
party on an ice cream sleigh.
This edible centerpiece can also
be made in individual servings.

This trompe l'oeil creation will surprise and delight both children and adults. Watch their puzzlement turn to smiles when the spaghetti dessert turns out to be ice cream.

ICE CREAM SPAGHETTI

Kids and adults alike will do a double take when they see this ice cream "pasta" with red sauce and "cheese" (see Note).

> ½ cup strawberry jelly
> 1 pint French Vanilla Ice Cream (see page 22), slightly softened
> ¼ cup white chocolate, chopped

1. Chill 4 dessert plates and a potato ricer. In a small bowl beat jelly with a fork until it liquifies.

2. Push ice cream slowly through chilled potato ricer. (If you use commercial ice cream, buy a standard, round, 1-pint carton; the ice cream will fit neatly, half at a time, into ricer.) Push one fourth of the ice cream onto each chilled plate. Pour one fourth of the jelly onto each serving of "pasta," sprinkle with chopped chocolate, and serve immediately.

Serves 4.

<u>Note</u> This dessert can be made ahead and frozen until serving time.

CHOCOLATE CHIP TUNNEL CAKE

Ice cream and cake are combined in this delicious dessert that is especially attractive when sliced. Coffee, mocha, and butter pecan ice creams work especially well.

> 1 cup sweetened condensed milk
> 2 ounces unsweetened chocolate, coarsely chopped
> ½ cup unsalted butter
> 1½ cups sugar
> 2 large eggs
> 1 teaspoon baking soda
> 1 cup milk
> 2½ cups flour
> 1 teaspoon vanilla extract
> 1 package (6 oz) chocolate chips
> 1 pint ice cream, any flavor, softened

1. Preheat oven to 350° F. Grease and flour a bundt pan.

2. In a heavy-bottomed saucepan over medium heat, boil condensed milk and chocolate, stirring constantly, until thick. Remove from heat and let cool.

3. In a medium bowl cream butter and sugar until light and fluffy. Add eggs one at a time, mixing well after each addition. Add cooled chocolate mixture.

4. Stir baking soda into milk and add to batter. Reserve 1 tablespoon flour; add the rest to batter and mix well. Stir in vanilla. Toss chocolate chips in the reserved flour and add.

5. Pour mixture into prepared bundt pan and bake until cake tester comes out clean when inserted (about 1¼ hours). Remove cake from pan and cool on wire rack.

6. When cake is completely cool, slice horizontally about one third of the way down from top. With a fork or spoon, dig a trench about 1½ inches deep in bottom layer. Fill trench with softened ice cream. Replace top layer, pressing down firmly. Wrap tightly and freeze. When sliced the cake will have an ice cream tunnel running through it.

Serves 8 to 10.

ICE CREAM SANDWICHES AND BARS

Combine homemade cookies and ice cream in a cold, crunchy sandwich for a special treat kids love to eat out of hand. Ice cream bars are another childhood delight. The bars in the recipes that follow are made like bar cookies and offer a quick variation on ice cream sandwiches. A crisp base is baked in a pan, layered with ice cream and a topping, frozen, then cut into bars.

OATMEAL–CHOCOLATE CHIP DELIGHTS

This sandwich is made with soft, chewy oatmeal cookies that won't shatter when you bite them.

- 1 cup rolled oats
- 1 cup flour
- 1 cup firmly packed light brown sugar
- ½ cup unsalted butter, melted
- 2 tablespoons boiling water
- 1 tablespoon corn syrup
- 1½ teaspoons baking soda
- 1 teaspoon vanilla extract
- ½ cup raisins
- 1 recipe Chocolate Chip Ice Cream (see page 22)

1. Preheat oven to 350° F. Lightly grease 2 baking sheets.

2. In a large bowl toss together oats, flour, and brown sugar. Stir in butter.

3. In a small bowl combine the water, corn syrup, baking soda, vanilla, and raisins. Add to oats mixture and knead lightly until dough comes together.

4. Shape dough into 18 balls about 1½ inches in diameter. Arrange balls on prepared baking sheets, leaving 1 inch for expansion. Flatten balls slightly. Bake until golden brown (10 to 12 minutes). Transfer to wire racks to cool.

5. Soften ice cream and assemble sandwiches as shown at right.

Makes 9 sandwiches.

SPICE BERRY SANDWICHES

The spicy cookies provide a counterpoint to the sweet berry ice cream.

- ¼ cup dried currants, finely chopped
- 2 tablespoons dark rum
- ¾ cup unsalted butter, softened
- ½ cup granulated sugar
- ¼ cup firmly packed dark brown sugar
- ¼ cup half-and-half
- 2 cups flour
- ½ teaspoon baking soda
- ½ teaspoon salt
- 1 teaspoon ground cinnamon
- ¼ teaspoon each *ground allspice, ginger, cloves, and cardamom*
- 2 ounces semisweet chocolate, finely chopped
- 1 recipe Fresh Berry Ice Cream (see page 40)

1. In a small bowl soak currants in rum for 10 minutes. Meanwhile, with an electric mixer, cream butter with sugars. Add half-and-half and beat until smooth.

2. Add flour, baking soda, salt, cinnamon, allspice, ginger, cloves, and cardamom. Blend well. Add chocolate and currant-rum mixture; blend well.

3. On a sheet of waxed paper, form dough into a log 2 inches in diameter. Wrap log in waxed paper and chill at least 2 hours.

4. Preheat oven to 350° F. Cut log into ¼-inch-thick slices. Place slices 1 inch apart on ungreased cookie sheet and bake until just firm to the touch (10 to 12 minutes). Transfer to wire racks to cool.

5. Soften ice cream and assemble sandwiches as shown at right.

Makes about 15 sandwiches.

ICE CREAM SANDWICHES

It takes just a few minutes to make a batch of ice cream sandwiches.

1. *Soften ice cream and put it into a pastry bag fitted with a large tip.*

2. *Pipe ice cream in spirals onto the flat side of half the cookies.*

3. *Place remaining cookies on top, pressing gently. Arrange sandwiches on a wire rack and freeze until firm. Wrap each sandwich in plastic wrap and store in freezer.*

CHOCOLATE–FRENCH VANILLA SANDWICHES

These chocolate wafers are worth the bit of extra effort they require.

- 4 ounces semisweet chocolate, chopped
- ⅓ cup unsweetened cocoa powder
- ⅓ cup water
- ¾ cup unsalted butter, at room temperature
- ¾ cup firmly packed light brown sugar
- ¾ cup granulated sugar
- 2 large eggs
- 1 tablespoon vanilla extract
- 2 cups flour
- 1 teaspoon baking soda
- 1 teaspoon boiling water
- 1 recipe French Vanilla Ice Cream (see page 22)

1. Melt chocolate in the top of a double boiler. In a small saucepan over medium heat, whisk together cocoa and the ⅓ cup water. Simmer, whisking constantly, until mixture is thick and the whisk leaves a trail across bottom of pan. Remove from heat, whisk in melted chocolate, and set aside.

2. With an electric mixer beat butter on medium-high speed until it whitens and holds soft peaks (3 to 5 minutes). Beat in sugars.

3. In a small bowl whisk together eggs and vanilla. Beat into butter mixture. Beat in chocolate mixture. Mix in 1 cup of the flour until just combined. Dissolve baking soda in the 1 teaspoon boiling water and beat in. Add remaining flour; mix only until well combined. Wrap dough in plastic wrap and freeze until firm. (This dough will never freeze solid. It is sticky; keeping it frozen makes it easier to work with.)

4. Preheat oven to 350° F. Divide dough into 4 equal parts. Return 3 parts to freezer. Roll remaining part between 2 sheets of plastic wrap into a rectangle about ¼ inch thick. Peel off one sheet of plastic wrap and invert dough onto a parchment-lined baking sheet. Peel off second sheet of plastic wrap and cut dough into 6 rectangles, each about 2 by 3 inches. Repeat with other 3 pieces of dough from freezer. Prick dough rectangles in an even pattern with the tines of a fork. (This is only for appearance.) Bake until cookies are slightly soft, but still spring back when touched (about 8 minutes). Cool on a wire rack.

5. Soften ice cream and assemble sandwiches as shown on page 57.

Makes 12 sandwiches.

CARAMEL CRUNCH BARS

The flavors in these bars go well with uncomplicated ice cream flavors, such as vanilla, strawberry, coffee, and chocolate.

- 1 cup flour
- ¼ cup regular oats, uncooked
- ½ cup chopped nuts, any kind
- ¼ cup firmly packed dark brown sugar
- ½ cup unsalted butter, at room temperature
- 1 recipe Old-Fashioned Butterscotch Sauce (see page 30)
- 1 quart ice cream, any flavor, softened

1. Preheat oven to 350° F. In a mixing bowl combine flour, oats, nuts, and brown sugar. Cut in butter with 2 knives until mixture resembles coarse meal. Transfer to a jelly-roll or similar pan and bake 20 minutes, stirring occasionally. Flour mixture will lightly brown, becoming fragrant as oats and nuts toast. Do not let it burn. Remove from oven and let cool.

2. Spread half of flour mixture in bottom of 8-inch-square baking pan. Spoon half of Old-Fashioned Butterscotch Sauce on top. Spread ice cream evenly over sauce. Top with remaining sauce and then with remaining flour mixture. Cover and freeze until firm.

3. With a sharp knife cut into bars approximately 2 by 2½ inches. Individually wrap and freeze bars not to be eaten immediately.

Makes 12 bars.

COCONUT BARS

This is a recipe that the kids can make themselves.

- 1 cup firmly packed light brown sugar
- 8 tablespoons unsalted butter
- 2 cups crushed cornflakes
- 1 cup chopped nuts, any kind
- 1½ cups coconut, toasted, shredded or flaked
- 1 quart French Vanilla Ice Cream (see page 22) or Coconut Ice Cream (see page 35), softened

1. In a small saucepan over medium heat, combine brown sugar and butter. Boil 1 minute. Place cornflakes in a bowl, pour hot butter mixture over them, and mix. Add nuts and coconut; mix well.

2. Press half the mixture into a 9-inch-square baking pan. Cover with ice cream. Top with remaining mixture. Wrap tightly and freeze.

3. With a sharp knife cut into 3- by 2¼-inch bars. Individually wrap bars that will not be eaten immediately and freeze until needed.

Makes 12 bars.

FROZEN BERRY BARS

Fresh berry, vanilla, or maple-walnut ice cream works well for these bars.

- 1 cup flour
- ¼ cup firmly packed light brown sugar
- ½ cup chopped nuts, any kind
- ½ cup unsalted butter, softened
- 1 cup whipping cream
- 2 large egg whites
- 1 cup granulated sugar
- 2 cups frozen berries, any kind, thawed and mashed
- 2 tablespoons lemon juice
- 1 quart ice cream, any flavor, softened

1. Preheat oven to 350° F. In a small bowl combine flour, brown sugar, nuts, and butter; mix well. Spread in a shallow pan and bake 20 minutes, stirring occasionally. Let cool.

2. In a large bowl whip the cream to soft peaks. Beat egg whites with an electric mixer until stiff peaks form. Fold granulated sugar, mashed berries, lemon juice, and whipped cream into beaten egg whites.

3. Sprinkle two thirds of the flour mixture over the bottom of a 9- by 13- by 2-inch baking pan. Spread ice cream on top. Spoon fruit mixture over ice cream and top with remaining flour mixture. Freeze; then cut into approximately 36 bars about 2 by 1½ inches.

Makes 36 bars.

FROZEN POPS

Frozen pops are simple to make and terrific to have on hand for the ever-hungry little ones. Yogurt, fruit juices, frozen berries, and frozen fruits all can contribute to your frozen-pop repertoire. You can buy plastic molds for freezing pops or simply use 3-, 4-, or 5-ounce paper cups. Always remember to partially freeze the pop mixture before adding the stick so the stick will remain upright.

YOGURT POPS

Match the yogurt flavor to the fruit or choose contrasting flavors.

> *2 cups yogurt, any flavor*
> *1 cup puréed fruit, any kind*
> *1 tablespoon honey*

Mix all ingredients together. Pour into molds and freeze until mixture is mushy. Insert stick and continue to freeze until pops are hard.

Makes 6 to 18 pops, depending on size of molds.

PUDDING POPS

These pops can be made from any pudding mix, instant or cooked.

> *1 package pudding mix*

1. Prepare pudding mix according to instructions on package.

2. While pudding is still pourable, pour it into five 4-ounce paper cups and freeze until firm but not hard (2 to 3 hours).

3. Insert a flat wooden ice cream stick into center of each pop and freeze overnight. To unmold, carefully tear off paper cups.

Makes 5 pops.

QUICK FRUIT POPS

Frozen fruit is transformed into a tasty snack on a stick.

> *2 cups frozen fruit (with or*
> *without syrup)*
> *1 cup water*
> *1 tablespoon sugar*

Thaw fruit slightly, then mix with the water and sugar. Pour into molds. Freeze until mixture is mushy. Insert sticks and continue to freeze until pops are hard.

Makes 6 to 18 pops, depending on size of molds.

Keep a supply of frozen pops in your freezer and you'll quickly become the neighborhood's favorite good humor person.

ICE CREAM PIZZA

Next birthday give the kids an ice cream pizza party. Make the pizza "crust" ahead. Just before serving, spread ice cream on the crust to look like melted cheese. Then let everyone at the party choose his or her own toppings. Let your (and your kids') imagination run wild.

TRIPLE-CHOCOLATE BROWNIE PIZZA

Based on a thick crust like a Chicago-style pizza, this will satisfy even the most ardent sweet tooth. The batter is a bowl-licker's delight.

   1 *pound semisweet chocolate, chopped*
   ¼ *cup unsweetened cocoa powder*
   4 *tablespoons unsalted butter*
   5 *large eggs*
   1½ *cups sugar*
   1½ *teaspoons vanilla extract*
   1 *cup sifted flour*
   ½ *teaspoon baking powder*
      Pinch of salt
   8 *ounces chocolate chips*
   8 *ounces walnuts or pecans, toasted and chopped (see Rocky Road Ice Cream, Note, page 22)*
   1 *recipe Peanut Butter Ice Cream (see page 25)*
   1 *recipe Mocha Ice Cream (see page 40)*
   1 *recipe Miss Jane Marble Sauce (see page 31)*
      Small bowls of assorted toppings, such as chopped peanuts, chopped nuts, sprinkles, jimmies, raisins, miniature chocolate chips, butterscotch chips, white chocolate chips, shredded coconut, granola, and candy pieces

1. Preheat oven to 350°F. Generously brush a 16-inch-diameter pizza pan with butter.

2. In a heavy-bottomed 1-quart saucepan over low heat, melt semisweet chocolate, cocoa, and butter, stirring until smooth. Remove from heat and let mixture cool about 5 minutes.

3. In a large bowl beat eggs and sugar with an electric mixer until thick and pale. Stir in vanilla and cooled chocolate mixture; blend well.

4. Combine flour, baking powder, and salt. Add to chocolate mixture, stirring just to combine. Fold in chocolate chips and nuts. Spread mixture in prepared pizza pan. Leave at least a ¼-inch border around edge to allow for expansion.

5. Bake about 30 minutes. The center will be quite moist inside (crumbs will adhere to a wooden toothpick inserted there). Let crust cool completely.

6. When crust is completely cool, spread with softened Peanut Butter Ice Cream. Cover surface with scoops of Mocha Ice Cream. Cut into wedges and serve. Allow each participant to select desired toppings from bowls. For a more impressive presentation, cover top of pizza with various toppings before bringing it to the table.

Serves 8 to 10.

Variations Other ice cream and topping combinations can be substituted for those above. Among the best are Banana-Rum Ice Cream (see page 36) with toasted coconut and chopped peanuts; White Chocolate Ice Cream (see page 40) with fresh raspberries and Vanilla Sauce (see page 30); and Peppermint-Stick Ice Cream (see page 23) with chocolate jimmies and sprinkles.

QUICK AND EASY ICE CREAM PIZZA

Strawberry jam spread over the crust of this pizza looks like tomato sauce. Small scoops of light-colored ice cream on top resemble mozzarella cheese.

   2 *packages (20 oz each) refrigerator cookie dough, such as sugar cookie, chocolate chip cookie, or chocolate brownie*
   1 *cup strawberry jam*
   1 *to 2 pints ice cream (flavor compatible with dough)*
      Toppings, such as jimmies and sprinkles

1. Preheat oven to 350° F. Line a 16-inch pizza pan with parchment.

2. Using a spatula or your lightly moistened fingertips, press chilled dough into an even layer in prepared pan. Bake until lightly browned (25 to 30 minutes). Let cool, then remove from pan and peel off paper.

3. When crust is completely cool, use a spatula to spread a layer of jam over it.

4. Either soften ice cream and spread a layer over "pizza crust" or cover crust with small scoops of ice cream. Add toppings.

Serves 8 to 10.

NUTTY BERRY PIZZA

This whimsical pizza is a cinch to prepare.

   10 *ounces slivered almonds, finely chopped*
   1 *cup unsalted butter, at room temperature*
   ⅓ *cup sugar*
   2½ *cups flour*
   1 *large egg, lightly beaten*
   1 *teaspoon almond extract*
   ½ *teaspoon vanilla extract*
   ⅛ *teaspoon salt*
   1 *recipe Fresh Berry Syrup (see page 26)*
   1 *recipe Fresh Berry Ice Cream (see page 40)*
   1 *cup chopped, toasted nuts, any kind (optional; see Rocky Road Ice Cream, Note, page 22)*

1. Preheat oven to 375° F. Butter a 16-inch-diameter pizza pan.

2. Combine almonds, butter, sugar, flour, egg, almond extract, vanilla, and salt. Mix well.

3. Press dough evenly into pan. Chill at least 30 minutes in refrigerator or 15 minutes in freezer.

4. Bake until crust is golden brown (about 20 minutes). Let cool.

5. With a spatula spread Fresh Berry Syrup over cooled crust. Top with small scoops of Fresh Berry Ice Cream, covering entire surface. Sprinkle chopped, toasted nuts over ice cream (if desired).

Serves 8 to 10.

A gala assortment of toppings makes this Triple-Chocolate Brownie Pizza a sure winner. Decorate it ahead or let your guests choose their own garnishes.

Refreshing Frozen Persimmon Cream served in Chocolate Shells (see page 82) is a stunning fall dessert, and an elegant way to end a special meal.

Celebrating the Seasons

The old adage "To everything there is a season" certainly applies to fresh fruits and vegetables. Thanks to sophisticated cultivation, storage, and transportation systems (including air freight for foreign-grown produce), we can get fresh fruit, even strawberries and blueberries, almost any time of year. Still, there is nothing like a perfect berry at its peak of ripeness, just picked, on a hot summer day. Ripe produce in season has a vibrant, exciting flavor that hothouse and cold-storage fruit can only hint at. As the fruits of each season come to market or ripen in your garden, capture their exquisite tastes in frozen desserts that intensify flavors by concentrating them and let you enjoy the moment of peak ripeness a little bit longer.

SPRING

When spring is bustin' out all over, luscious blood oranges, mangoes, apricots, and other spring fruits make their welcome appearance. So shake off the last of the winter blahs with a stunning Blood Orange Sorbet (see page 65) or a Frozen Mascarpone Cream with Ginger-Mango Sauce (below), guaranteed to satisfy the most demanding sweet tooth. If winter eating has expanded your waistline, fragrant Minted Pink Grapefruit Ice (see page 73) will start you on your way to lighter warm-weather eating.

FROZEN MASCARPONE CREAM WITH GINGER-MANGO SAUCE

Mascarpone is a rich, unripened, very soft Italian cheese. It is offset in this dessert by the sharpness of ginger.

- 4 *large egg yolks*
- ⅓ *cup sugar*
- 1 *pound mascarpone cheese*
- 2 *tablespoons dark rum*
- 1 *cup whipping cream*

Ginger-Mango Sauce

- 2 *pounds whole mangoes, peeled, pitted, and diced*
- 3 *teaspoons sugar, or to taste*
- ¼ *cup finely chopped candied ginger*
- 1 *to 2 teaspoons lemon juice*

1. In a large bowl beat egg yolks until light yellow. Beat in sugar and continue beating until mixture is pale and light. Blend in mascarpone and rum. Stir in cream until well blended. Pour into a lightly oiled 4-cup loaf pan, wrap well, and freeze until firm.

2. To serve, cut frozen cream into ½-inch-thick slices and top with Ginger-Mango Sauce.

Serves 8.

Ginger-Mango Sauce Reserve about ½ cup of the diced mango. Place remaining mango in a food processor or blender and purée until smooth. Spoon purée into a bowl and stir in reserved mango, sugar, candied ginger, and lemon juice.

Makes about 2 cups.

PAPAYA ICE CREAM

When choosing a papaya, look for one with yellow skin. Green on the skin is an indication that the fruit is not yet ripe. The papayas must be heated to inactivate an enzyme that would otherwise break down the proteins in the milk and cream and cause a bitter taste.

- 2 *large papayas*
- 2 *cups milk*
- 2 *cups whipping cream*
- ½ *cup sugar*
- 4 *large egg yolks*
- 2 *tablespoons fresh lime juice*

1. Cut papayas in half, scoop out flesh, and discard skin and seeds. Finely chop fruit. Warm it in a small, heavy-bottomed saucepan over very low heat, stirring occasionally, about 15 minutes. Remove from heat and let cool.

2. In a heavy-bottomed 2-quart saucepan, heat milk, cream, and sugar, stirring occasionally, until sugar is dissolved and mixture is hot but not boiling. Lightly whisk egg yolks in a bowl. Keep whisking and very slowly pour in approximately 1 cup of the cream mixture.

3. When egg mixture is smooth, pour it back into pan with cream and cook, whisking constantly, until it thickens slightly and coats the back of a spoon (about 5 minutes). Be careful not to let mixture boil, or it will curdle. Strain into a clean bowl and let cool.

4. Stir in prepared papaya and lime juice. Transfer to an ice cream machine and freeze according to manufacturer's instructions.

Makes about 1 quart.

BURNT-ALMOND AND APRICOT ICE CREAM WITH APRICOT SAUCE

This is a dessert for apricot lovers, with fresh apricots in the ice cream and dried apricots, plus a splash of apricot brandy, in the sauce.

- 2 *cups fresh apricots, peeled, pitted, and chopped*
- ⅓ *cup amaretto*
- ½ *cup sugar*
- 1 *cup slivered almonds*
- 1 *recipe French Vanilla Ice Cream Base I (see page 13)*

Apricot Sauce

- 3 *ounces dried apricots, chopped (about ½ cup firmly packed)*
- 1½ *cups water*
- ⅓ *cup sugar*
- 3 *tablespoons apricot brandy or Cognac*
- ¼ *cup apricot nectar*

1. In a food processor or blender, purée apricots with amaretto.

2. In a small, heavy-bottomed skillet, cook sugar over moderate heat, stirring with a wooden spoon, until just melted and starting to caramelize. Immediately remove from heat. Fold in almonds and pour onto a sheet of waxed paper. Cool to room temperature.

3. Place a sheet of waxed paper over cooled almonds and lightly crush with a rolling pin. Add apricot purée and crushed almonds to ice cream base. Transfer to an ice cream machine and freeze according to manufacturer's instructions. Serve topped with Apricot Sauce.

Makes about 1⅓ quarts.

Apricot Sauce Combine apricots, the water, and sugar in a small, heavy-bottomed saucepan and cook over low heat until sugar is dissolved. Increase heat to medium and simmer until apricots are very soft and liquid is reduced to a thick syrup (about 20 minutes). Stir frequently during last 5 minutes to prevent burning. Remove from heat and let cool. Add brandy and apricot nectar. Refrigerate until needed.

Makes about 1½ cups.

FROZEN CHOCOLATE FROMAGE

This very rich dessert resembles a frozen chocolate cheesecake. Fresh orange slices are a good accompaniment.

6 ounces cream cheese, at
  room temperature
2 large egg yolks
2 tablespoons sugar
½ teaspoon vanilla extract
1 tablespoon coffee-
  flavored liqueur
½ cup whipping cream
3 ounces semisweet chocolate,
  melted
½ cup slivered almonds, toasted
  (see Rocky Road Ice Cream,
  Note, page 22)

1. In a food processor or blender, mix together cream cheese, egg yolks, sugar, vanilla, liqueur, and cream. When well mixed, blend in melted chocolate. Mix in almonds.

2. Transfer to a 2-cup bowl or four ½-cup dessert dishes (bowls, ramekins, or small parfait dishes) and freeze until firm. Let stand at room temperature for 5 minutes before serving. If frozen in a large bowl, serve with an ice cream scoop.

Serves 4.

BLOOD ORANGE SORBET

The unusual, striking color and exceptional citrus flavor of blood oranges make this sorbet a beautiful addition to your dessert menu. Now that blood oranges are being grown in the United States, they are plentiful and reasonably priced.

1 cup sugar
1 cup water
2 cups blood orange juice

1. In a small saucepan bring sugar and the water to a boil, then simmer 5 minutes. Set aside to cool about 10 minutes.

2. Combine sugar syrup with blood orange juice and chill well. Transfer to an ice cream machine and freeze according to manufacturer's instructions.

Makes 1½ pints.

LEMON SHERBET WITH BLACK WALNUT BRITTLE CUPS

The distinctive taste of black walnuts is a perfect foil for tart lemon sherbet. It is best to store walnuts in the freezer, because they can turn rancid quickly. Refresh them before use by heating them in a moderate oven for a few minutes.

¾ cup fresh lemon juice (about
  6 lemons)
½ cup superfine sugar
2½ cups whole or low-fat milk
  Zest of 2 lemons,
  finely chopped

Black Walnut Brittle Cups

1 cup sugar
1⅓ cups black walnuts: ⅔ cup
  coarsley chopped, ⅔ cup
  finely chopped
1 pound semisweet chocolate,
  coarsely chopped

In a medium bowl mix lemon juice and sugar. Stir in milk and zest all at once (the milk will curdle slightly); mix well. Transfer to an ice cream machine and freeze according to manufacturer's instructions. Serve with Black Walnut Brittle Cups.

Makes about 1 quart.

Black Walnut Brittle Cups

1. In a small, heavy-bottomed saucepan, cook sugar over medium heat until melted, stirring constantly. Remove from heat and immediately add coarsely chopped black walnuts. Pour quickly into 36 small foil nut cups. Cool.

2. In a small, heavy-bottomed saucepan, melt chocolate over low heat. Divide melted chocolate among prepared nut cups. Sprinkle tops with finely chopped black walnuts. Let cool.

Makes 3 dozen walnut cups.

RASPBERRY SHERBET IN CHOCOLATE CUPS

Chocolate and raspberry is one of the all-time-great combinations, providing delightful contrasts in color, texture, and taste.

2 cups fresh raspberries
1 cup sugar
1 cup sour cream
½ teaspoon vanilla extract
  Fresh mint leaves, for garnish
  (optional)

Chocolate Cups

½ pound semisweet chocolate,
  coarsely chopped
2 tablespoons unsalted butter

In a large bowl mash raspberries and sugar together; let stand 1 hour. Add sour cream and vanilla; mix well. Transfer to an ice cream machine and freeze according to manufacturer's instructions. To serve, scoop into Chocolate Cups. Garnish, if desired, with fresh mint leaves.

Makes about 12 servings.

Chocolate Cups In the top of a double boiler, melt chocolate and butter together. Remove from heat and cool slightly. Line muffin pans with paper baking cups. Paint inside of cups with a thin coating of chocolate. Chill until firm. Peel off paper and fill cups with raspberry sherbet.

Makes 12 to 16 Chocolate Cups.

Celebrate the first fruits and flowers of spring with this sophisticated Frozen Mango Mousse, served in crisp Coconut Tulips.

FROZEN MANGO MOUSSE IN COCONUT TULIPS

Crunchy coconut cups serve as elegant edible dishes for this creamy-smooth, rum-spiked mousse.

> 5 large ripe mangoes, peeled,
>   pitted, and chopped
> 7 tablespoons dark rum
> 1 cup sugar
> ½ cup water
> 2 large egg whites
> 1 cup whipping cream
> 1 tablespoon lime juice

Coconut Tulips

> 1 small coconut (see Note)
> ½ cup unsalted butter
> ½ cup sugar
> ½ cup flour
> 1 teaspoon finely grated
>   lemon zest
> ¼ teaspoon each ground
>   cinnamon and ground cloves
> 1 large egg white, at
>   room temperature

1. Place chopped mangoes in a food processor or blender and purée. Remove ½ cup of the purée; set aside. Add 5 tablespoons of the rum to remaining purée and mix well.

2. In a small, heavy-bottomed saucepan, mix ¾ cup of the sugar with the water and bring to a boil over moderate heat. Simmer to soft-ball stage (238° F; see page 16). Meanwhile, beat egg whites to soft peaks. While beating constantly add hot sugar syrup in a thin, steady stream. Continue to beat until glossy and stiff (about 5 minutes).

3. Whip the cream to stiff peaks. Fold rum-flavored mango purée into meringue and then fold in whipped cream. Spoon mixture into a freezer container and freeze until firm (at least 4 hours).

4. To make topping for mousse, in a small saucepan combine reserved purée, remaining sugar, remaining rum, and lime juice. Cook over low heat until sugar is dissolved. Remove from heat, let cool, and refrigerate.

5. To serve, scoop mango mousse into coconut tulips; drizzle topping over mousse.

Makes about 1 quart.

Coconut Tulips

1. Preheat oven to 350° F. Line a baking sheet with lightly buttered parchment paper. Have ready 6 overturned 4-ounce ramekins or 6 small (2-inch-diameter bottom) bowls.

2. Open coconut, reserving liquid; remove and grate or finely shred meat (see photographs at right).

3. Melt butter in a small, heavy-bottomed saucepan over low heat. When foam subsides stir in sugar and cook 1 minute. Remove from heat, stir in flour, ½ cup of the grated coconut, and 1 tablespoon of the reserved coconut juice. Stir until smooth. Stir in lemon zest, cinnamon, and cloves.

4. Beat egg white to soft peaks. Fold one fourth of beaten whites into batter to lighten it, then gently fold in remaining whites.

5. On prepared baking sheet form batter into three to six 4-inch-diameter circles (depending on size of sheet), at least 3 inches apart and 1 inch from sides of sheet. Use 2 tablespoons batter for each circle. Spread batter with a spatula if necessary. Bake until edges are deep golden brown (10 to 13 minutes).

6. Let cookies cool on baking sheet 30 seconds, then remove one at a time with a large metal spatula. Working quickly, drape each cookie over an overturned ramekin. Mold cookie gently over ramekin to form a tulip shape. Allow each tulip to set 2 minutes, then transfer to a wire rack to cool. Repeat baking and shaping with remaining batter. Place finished tulips on a baking sheet in the freezer until ready to use.

Makes 8 to 10.

Note Fresh coconut is essential for the flavor it gives these crisp creations.

CONQUERING A FRESH COCONUT

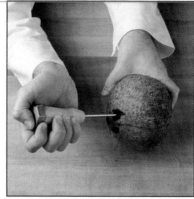

1. *Pierce the eyes of the coconut with an ice pick. Drain the liquid into a bowl through a sieve lined with a double layer of cheesecloth.*

2. *Bake until the shell cracks (about 15 minutes at 350°–375° F). Tap the coconut shell with a hammer until it splits all the way open.*

3. *Pry the meat from the shell with a sturdy (not sharp) knife. Pare the brown skin from the coconut meat.*

SPRINGTIME IS FOR LOVERS

California Seviche

*Double-Mushroom Chicken Breasts
With Madeira*

Sautéed Spring Vegetables

Rice Pilaf

*Coeur à la Crème Fraîche Ice Cream
With Fresh Berries*

*Suggested beverage: Champagne
or chilled mineral water
with a splash of Raspberry Syrup
(see Fresh Berry Syrup, page 26)*

*Spring is the season of
sentimental notions, new
beginnings, abundant
flowers, and the first berries
of the year. What a perfect
time to launch a new
romance or rekindle an
existing one. This year,
celebrate spring with that
special someone and this
romantic menu for two.
The appropriately
heart-shaped dessert is a
frozen twist on an old
French classic.*

CALIFORNIA SEVICHE

This light, refreshing appetizer must
be made at least 5 hours before
serving.

   8 ounces white-fleshed fish,
     such as tilefish, rockfish, or
     red snapper
   3 limes: 2 large juiced,
     1 medium whole
   1 medium tomato, peeled,
     seeded, and chopped
   1 small jalapeño or serrano
     chile, seeded and chopped
   2 tablespoons olive oil
     Kosher salt and freshly
     ground pepper, to taste
   2 green onions, finely chopped
   2 tablespoons chopped cilantro
   1 avocado, peeled, seeded,
     and sliced, for garnish

1. Remove skin and bones from fish;
cut flesh into ½-inch cubes. Place in
a medium-sized glass bowl and cover
with lime juice. Cover bowl and
refrigerate until fish turns opaque (at
least 5 hours).

2. Drain off juice and combine cubed
fish with tomato, chile, oil, salt,
pepper, onion, and cilantro. Squeeze
lime over mixture and toss. Arrange
sliced avocado on top and serve.

DOUBLE-MUSHROOM CHICKEN BREASTS WITH MADEIRA

These can be prepared early in the
day and cooked when needed.

   1 whole chicken breast, halved,
     boned, skin on
     Salt, to taste
     Paprika, to taste
   1 tablespoon olive oil
   ¼ cup Madeira wine
   1 tablespoon unsalted butter
   ¼ pound fresh mushrooms,
     thinly sliced
   ¾ cup whipping cream

Mushroom Duxelles

   2 tablespoons unsalted butter
   1 shallot, finely chopped
   ¼ pound fresh mushrooms,
     finely chopped
   1 tablespoon flour
   ¼ cup whipping cream

   ¼ teaspoon salt
     Pinch of cayenne pepper
   1 tablespoon finely chopped
     fresh parsley
   1½ teaspoons finely chopped
     fresh chives
   ¼ teaspoon lemon juice

1. Preheat oven to 350° F. Grease a
shallow pan that can be used both in
oven and on top of stove.

2. Wash chicken and pat dry.
Sprinkle with salt and paprika. Lay
each half breast skin side up on a
cutting board. Loosen skin by gently
sliding your fingertips between skin
and meat.

3. Insert half of Mushroom Duxelles
under skin of each breast, concentrating filling in middle of breast.
Fold under skin and meat to form
dome. Brush with oil.

4. Place stuffed breasts skin side up
in prepared pan. Bake on center rack
of oven for 30 minutes.

5. Remove breasts to a warm platter;
cover with foil. Discard all but
1 teaspoon of the fat in pan. Place
pan on top of stove over medium
heat, add Madeira wine, and reduce
by one half. With a spatula loosen
any bits of chicken that cling to pan.
Swirl in butter, then add mushrooms
and quickly sauté. Pour in cream and
continue to cook, stirring constantly,
until cream thickens enough to coat
the back of a spoon. Adjust seasoning.
Serve over chicken breasts.

Mushroom Duxelles

1. Melt butter in a medium-sized
sauté pan. Add shallot and cook
slowly until soft but not brown. Stir
in mushrooms. Cook over medium
heat, stirring occasionally, until
all moisture has evaporated (10 to
15 minutes).

2. Sprinkle flour over mushrooms
and incorporate completely by stirring for 1 or 2 minutes. Pour cream
into pan and mix thoroughly while
bringing to a boil. Remove from heat.

3. Stir in salt, cayenne, parsley,
chives, and lemon juice. Refrigerate
until needed.

Lavish crème fraîche ice cream, shaped in a traditional coeur à la crème mold, is a fitting finale for a springtime dinner for lovers.

RICE PILAF

This versatile rice dish is good any time of the year.

- 2 tablespoons unsalted butter
- 1 tablespoon pine nuts
- ½ small onion, chopped
- ¾ cup long-grain rice
- ½ teaspoon salt
- 2 cups chicken stock, boiling

1. Melt 1 tablespoon of the butter in a heavy-bottomed 1½ quart saucepan. Add nuts and sauté until they turn light brown. Remove with a slotted spoon and reserve. Add onion to pan and sauté until soft and starting to turn golden. Remove and combine with pine nuts.

2. Melt remaining butter in pan. Add rice and sauté until golden. Return nuts and onion to pan.

3. Add salt to broth and pour over rice mixture. Bring to a boil. Cover and simmer very slowly until rice is tender and liquid has been completely absorbed (about 20 minutes).

4. Remove pan from heat and allow to sit, covered, about 5 minutes. Fluff with a fork before serving.

COEUR À LA CRÈME FRAÎCHE ICE CREAM WITH FRESH BERRIES

Here is a heart-shaped treat for you and your sweetheart—with just enough left over for seconds. Serve it alone or with Chocolate Madeleines (see page 47). Crème Fraîche, France's slightly sour, nutty-tasting cream, must ripen for at least 8 hours and be refrigerated for 4 hours before using. Storebought crème fraîche (available in many gourmet shops) can be substituted.

- 5 large egg yolks
- 1 cup sugar
- 1 cup whipping cream
- ½ teaspoon vanilla extract
- 1 pint fresh strawberries, washed and hulled
- ½ cup Raspberry Purée (see page 112), for topping

Crème Fraîche

- 1 tablespoon buttermilk
- 1 cup whipping cream

1. Lightly whisk egg yolks in a medium bowl. Add Crème Fraîche, sugar, cream, and vanilla, mixing well. Transfer to an ice cream machine and freeze according to manufacturer's instructions. When almost frozen, transfer ice cream to a heart-shaped mold lined with plastic wrap. Freeze until firm.

2. Unmold heart onto chilled platter. Surround with fresh strawberries. Drizzle raspberry purée over top.

Crème Fraîche In a small saucepan combine buttermilk and cream. Warm over medium heat to about 90° F. Pour into a glass jar, cover loosely, and let stand in a warm place until thick (8 to 24 hours). Cover tightly and refrigerate at least 4 hours before using.

Makes about 1 cup.

RHUBARB CRUNCH WITH RHUBARB ICE CREAM

Here is a good way to take advantage of fresh rhubarb when it is plentiful in the spring.

- 1 cup flour
- 1 cup firmly packed light brown sugar
- ¾ cup regular oatmeal, uncooked
- ½ cup unsalted butter, melted
- 4 cups diced rhubarb
- ½ cup granulated sugar
- 2 tablespoons cornstarch
- 1 cup water
- 2 teaspoons vanilla extract

Rhubarb Ice Cream

- ¾ cup sugar
- 3 cups chopped rhubarb
- 2 teaspoons lemon juice
- 3 to 4 drops red food coloring (optional)
- 1 recipe French Vanilla Ice Cream Base I (see page 13)

1. Preheat oven to 350° F. Mix together flour, brown sugar, oatmeal, and melted butter until crumbly. Press half the mixture into bottom of an 8-inch-square pan. Top with rhubarb.

2. In a small saucepan combine granulated sugar, cornstarch, the water, and vanilla. Cook until thick and clear. Pour over rhubarb and top with remaining crumb mixture. Bake 1 hour. Serve warm, topping each serving with a generous scoop of Rhubarb Ice Cream.

Serves 12 to 14.

Rhubarb Ice Cream Sprinkle sugar over rhubarb; toss to coat fruit. Place in a medium saucepan, cover, and cook over moderate heat, stirring once or twice, until rhubarb is soft (about 10 minutes). Remove from heat. Add lemon juice and food coloring (if used). When cool remove rhubarb with a slotted spoon; finely chop and add to ice cream base. Transfer to an ice cream machine and freeze according to manufacturer's instructions.

Makes about 1 quart.

FROZEN LEMON SOUFFLÉ

This dessert is the perfect ending to a rich meal.

- 1 tablespoon unflavored gelatin
- ¼ cup cold water
- 6 egg yolks and 4 egg whites, extra large
- 1 cup sugar
- ⅔ cup lemon juice
  Zest of 1 lemon, finely chopped
- 1½ cups whipping cream

1. Prepare a 2-quart soufflé dish by wrapping a 3-inch-wide strip of aluminum foil around top edge to form a collar. Tape in place.

2. Soften gelatin in the cold water. Set aside. In a medium saucepan beat egg yolks and sugar together until light colored and creamy. Add lemon juice and cook over low heat, stirring constantly, until thick. Add softened gelatin and lemon zest, stirring well to dissolve gelatin. Cool.

3. Whip the cream to soft peaks. In another bowl beat egg whites to soft peaks. Fold cream into egg yolk mixture, then fold in egg whites. Transfer to soufflé dish and freeze at least 4 hours before serving.

Serves 8 to 10.

FRESH FRUIT SHELLS

On special occasions you can dress up sorbets by serving them frozen in the fruits from which they were made. Hollowed-out lemons, limes, Granny Smith apples, kiwifruits, mangoes, guavas, plums, peaches, oranges, apricots, and giant strawberries make perfect serving containers. Simply scoop out the centers of the fruits, freeze the shells, then fill with the appropriate sorbets. Wrap tightly and return to the freezer until time for serving.

For an especially festive presentation, line a large grapevine basket with moss or leaves and decorate it with such flowers as sweet peas, roses, nasturtiums, and honeysuckle. Arrange the sorbet-filled frozen fruits in the basket and let your guests pick out their favorites. Use the basic sorbet recipe on page 15 and let your imagination run wild.

You can add a dash of liqueur in the flavor of each sorbet or a complementary flavor to give the sorbets extra sparkle. The following combinations work very well: lime sorbet with tequila, apricot sorbet with amaretto or apricot brandy, peach sorbet with rum, strawberry sorbet with white crème de menthe, plum sorbet with kirsch, orange sorbet with Cointreau, apple sorbet with calvados, pear sorbet with pear liqueur, lemon sorbet with vodka or gin, kiwifruit sorbet with Reisling wine.

Three unlikely ice cream flavors—tomato, garlic, and avocado—taste great singly or in combination. What's for dessert tonight? Guacamole!

AVOCADO ICE CREAM

This lovely pale green ice cream has an elusive but very pleasant flavor. The most flavorful avocado to use is the pebbly-textured Hass variety.

> 2 cups whipping cream
> 2 cups whole milk
> ¾ cup sugar
> 4 large egg yolks
> 1 large ripe avocado, peeled, pit removed (see Note)
> 3 tablespoons fresh lemon juice

1. In a heavy-bottomed 2-quart saucepan, heat cream, milk, and sugar. Stir occasionally until sugar is dissolved and mixture is hot but not boiling.

2. Whisk egg yolks together in a bowl. Keep whisking and very slowly pour in 1 cup of the cream mixture. When smooth, pour back into pan of hot liquid and cook, whisking constantly, until mixture thickens slightly and coats the back of a spoon (about 5 minutes). Be careful not to let mixture boil, or it will curdle. Strain into a clean bowl and cool thoroughly.

3. Purée avocado meat with lemon juice. Add to strained mixture. Transfer to an ice cream machine and freeze according to manufacturer's instructions.

Makes about 1 quart.

Note If you wish to reserve the avocado skin to use as two dishes for ice cream, cut the avocado in half from stem to base, cutting around the outside of the fruit to avoid the pit. Twist the halves in opposite directions to separate. After removing pit and meat, rinse the shells and refrigerate until serving time.

GARLIC ICE CREAM

You'll have to try it to believe it.

> 1½ cups whipping cream
> ½ cup milk
> ⅓ cup sugar
> 1 large clove garlic, crushed
> Pinch of salt
> 2 large egg yolks
> 1 tablespoon honey
> 1 teaspoon lemon juice

1. In a heavy-bottomed saucepan heat cream, milk, sugar, garlic, and salt, stirring occasionally, until sugar is melted and mixture is hot but not boiling.

2. Whisk egg yolks together in a bowl. Keep whisking and very slowly pour in 1 cup of the cream mixture. When smooth, pour back into pan of hot liquid. Cook, whisking constantly, until mixture thickens slightly and coats the back of a spoon (about 5 minutes). Be careful not to let mixture boil, or it will curdle. Strain into a clean bowl. Add honey and lemon juice, mixing well. Cool thoroughly.

3. Transfer to an ice cream machine and freeze according to manufacturer's instructions.

Makes about 1½ pints.

TOMATO ICE CREAM

Tell your friends that it's "Love Apple" ice cream.

> 1½ cups whipping cream
> ½ cup milk
> ⅓ cup sugar
> 1 tablespoon tomato paste
> ½ cup strained tomato purée
> 2 large egg yolks
> 1 teaspoon vanilla extract
> Pinch of salt

1. In a medium-sized, heavy-bottomed saucepan, heat cream, milk, sugar, tomato paste, and tomato purée, stirring occasionally, until sugar is dissolved and mixture is hot but not boiling.

2. Whisk egg yolks together in a small bowl. Keep whisking and pour in 1 cup of the cream mixture. When smooth, pour back into pan of hot liquid and cook, whisking constantly, until mixture thickens slightly and coats the back of a spoon (about 5 minutes). Be careful not to let mixture boil, or it will curdle. Strain into a clean bowl and cool thoroughly. Add vanilla and salt.

3. Transfer to an ice cream machine and freeze according to manufacturer's instructions.

Makes about 1 pint.

MINTED PINK GRAPEFRUIT ICE

This easy-to-prepare, delicately flavored dessert is the perfect finale for a light lunch.

> ⅔ cup sugar
> 3 large pink grapefruits, peeled and sectioned, membrane removed
> 2 tablespoons white crème de menthe
> ¼ cup water
> Mint leaves, for garnish

Combine sugar, grapefruit sections, crème de menthe, and the water in a food processor or blender and purée. Transfer to an ice cream machine and freeze according to manufacturer's instructions. Serve in chilled dessert dishes, garnished with fresh mint leaves.

Makes about 1 pint.

Beer Sorbet With Chocolate Pretzels puts a whole new twist on pretzels and beer for summertime refreshment and fun.

SUMMER

A great delight of summer is the fresh fruit that comes into its own as soon as the days grow long and sunny. Plump berries, fragrant peaches, sweet-tart plums—all seem to reach their peaks at once. Their dazzling colors and rich, round flavors make for memorable frozen desserts.

PEACHES-AND-CREAM MOUSSE

Few can resist the taste of peaches and cream.

  8 *ripe peaches, peeled,*
     pitted, and chopped
  3 *tablespoons fresh lemon juice*
  2 *teaspoons vanilla extract*
  ½ *cup sugar*
  2 *cups Crème Fraîche*
     (see page 70)

Combine peaches, lemon juice, vanilla, and sugar. Purée in a food processor or blender until smooth. Fold into Crème Fraîche. Pour into ten 4- or 5-ounce ramekins. Freeze.

Serves 10.

FROZEN NECTARINE TORTE

Peaches or plums also work well in this quick and easy dessert.

  2 *pounds ripe nectarines, peeled,*
     stoned, and chopped
  1 *cup sugar*
  1 *tablespoon lemon juice*
  1 *cup whipping cream*
  1 *cup macaroon crumbs*

Mash prepared nectarines with sugar and lemon juice, mixing well. Whip the cream to soft peaks and fold into nectarines. Sprinkle ½ cup of the macaroon crumbs into the bottom of a 1-quart bowl. Pour in nectarine mixture and top with remaining crumbs. Freeze until firm.

Serves 8.

BEER SORBET WITH CHOCOLATE PRETZELS

Capture the effervescence of your favorite beer in this cooling, light dessert. The chocolate-dipped pretzels are a perfect counterpoint.

>   1   bottle (12 oz) beer,
>   well chilled
> 1½   cups Simple Sugar Syrup
>   (see page 15)
>   1   tablespoon lime juice

Chocolate Pretzels

>   8   ounces bittersweet chocolate,
>   coarsely chopped
>   1   bag (16 oz) pretzels

Combine beer, syrup, and lime juice. Transfer to an ice cream machine and freeze according to manufacturer's instructions.

Makes about 3 cups.

Chocolate Pretzels Melt chocolate in the top of a double boiler. Dip in half of each pretzel. Let dry on wire racks. Store in an airtight container in a cool place.

Makes about 40 pretzels.

PLUM AND ZINFANDEL ICE

Serve this deep purple cooler on warm evenings.

>   2   pounds fresh plums, pitted
>   and chopped
> 1½   cups Zinfandel wine
>   ½   cup water
>   1   cup sugar
>   1   cinnamon stick

1. In a large saucepan combine all ingredients. Bring to a boil over medium heat. Reduce heat and simmer until plums are very tender (about 20 minutes). Skim off any foam that has formed.

2. Cool slightly and discard cinnamon stick. Purée cooked plums with their liquid in a food processor or blender, then strain through a large-holed sieve or put through a food mill fitted with a medium blade. Transfer to an ice cream machine and freeze according to manufacturer's instructions.

Makes about 1 quart.

FROZEN CHERRY SOUFFLÉ WITH CHERRY CHUTNEY

Freeze cherries when they are plentiful, and this summer treat can be a year-round favorite. The chutney is so good you will also want to use it as a condiment with grilled foods.

>   2   pounds fresh dark cherries,
>   stemmed and pitted
> 1¼   cups sugar
>   ½   cup water
>   6   large egg whites, at
>   room temperature
>   1   cup whipping cream

Cherry Chutney

>   1   to 1½ pounds dark cherries
>   (3 cups) stemmed and pitted
> 1½   cups cider vinegar
>   1   cup chopped onion
>   ¾   cup sugar
>   ¾   cup golden raisins
>   3   tablespoons minced
>   candied ginger
>   3   teaspoons mustard seed
>   1   teaspoon ground cinnamon
>   ½   teaspoon salt
>   ¼   teaspoon each *ground
>   allspice, ground cloves, and
>   ground nutmeg*

1. In a heavy-bottomed medium-sized saucepan, crush cherries with ¼ cup of the sugar. Heat, stirring constantly, over medium-low heat until cherries are soft and liquid thickens slightly. Cool and purée in food processor or blender.

2. Prepare a 4-cup soufflé dish: Cut a piece of aluminum foil long enough to fit around dish and overlap by 2 inches. Fold in half lengthwise and wrap around dish to form a collar extending about 2½ inches above rim of dish. Tie foil in place with string.

3. Cook remaining sugar and the water in a small, heavy-bottomed saucepan over medium heat, stirring until sugar dissolves. Cook to soft-ball stage (238° F; see page 16). While

sugar cooks beat egg whites until stiff but not dry. To make meringue continue beating and pour syrup into whites in a thin, steady steam. Beat until meringue is very light and fluffy and feels cool to the touch.

4. Whip cream to soft peaks. Fold cherry purée into meringue, then fold in whipped cream. Pour mixture into prepared soufflé dish and freeze until firm. To serve, spoon into dessert bowls and top with Cherry Chutney.

Serves 8.

Cherry Chutney Combine all ingredients in a large, heavy-bottomed saucepan. Bring to a boil and simmer, covered, 1 hour. Simmer uncovered, stirring occasionally until thickened (about 30 minutes more). Remove from heat, let cool, and chill until needed.

Makes about 3 cups.

SUMMER-FRUIT RAGOUT

This is a richly flavorful sauce to be spooned over ice cream. Heartier fruits are added at the beginning of the cooking process; the most fragile are added at the last moment to barely warm through.

>   3   peaches, peeled, stoned,
>   and sliced
>   3   nectarines, peeled, stoned,
>   and sliced
>   3   cups Riesling or other
>   sweet white wine
>   Pinch of salt
>   3   tablespoons unsalted butter
>   2   cups assorted fresh berries,
>   such as blackberries, blue-
>   berries, and raspberries

1. In a large sauté pan over medium heat, simmer peaches and nectarines in wine until fruit is tender. Remove with a slotted spoon and keep warm. Turn heat to high and reduce poaching liquid by half.

2. Remove from heat, add salt, and swirl in butter. Return poached fruit to pan, add berries, and stir until berries are just warmed through.

3. Spoon over ice cream. Refrigerate leftovers; gently reheat before using.

Makes about 1 quart.

75

FOURTH OF JULY BACKYARD GRILL

*Swordfish Brochette
With Honey-Mustard Sauce*

G. Lee's Baked Hush Puppies

Yankee Doodle Coleslaw

Corn on the Cob

Sliced Tomatoes

Frozen Watermelon Bombe

*Suggested beverage: cold beer
or iced tea with lemon*

By combining make-ahead recipes with last-minute outdoor grilling, this holiday menu offers lots of good food for family and friends and plenty of time for fun. Make the honey-mustard sauce, soubise, coleslaw, and Frozen Watermelon Bombe a day or two in advance. The morning of the party, simply slice the tomatoes, husk the corn, and make the hush puppies. Then you'll be able to relax and enjoy your guests until it's time to put the fish on the grill.

SWORDFISH BROCHETTE WITH HONEY-MUSTARD SAUCE

A brochette is usually served on a bed of rice; this recipe uses delicious Onion and Rice Soubise instead.

    4 swordfish steaks (6 oz each),
       each cut into 6 to 8
       equal pieces
    1 cup whipping cream
    3 tablespoons dry white wine
    1 tablespoon honey
    1 tablespoon coarse-grained
       mustard

Onion and Rice Soubise

    5 tablespoons unsalted butter
    2 pounds white onions,
       peeled and coarsely sliced
    ¾ cup rice
    2 cups fish or chicken stock
    1 teaspoon salt
    ½ teaspoon freshly ground
       white pepper
    ⅓ cup whipping cream

1. Preheat grill. Skewer fish pieces.

2. In a small saucepan over medium-high heat, reduce cream by half. Watch carefully to prevent cream from boiling over. Add wine, honey, and mustard. Mix well. Simmer 1 minute. Remove from heat.

3. Brush skewered fish with sauce. Place on grill and cook 3 to 5 minutes, turning once. Serve with remaining sauce on a bed of Onion and Rice Soubise.

Serves 4 to 6.

Onion and Rice Soubise Melt 3 tablespoons of the butter in a large saucepan, add onions, and cook until soft but not brown (5 to 7 minutes). Add rice and mix well; then add stock, salt, and pepper. Cover and simmer 30 minutes. Purée in a food processor or blender with cream and remaining butter. Reheat over low heat. Adjust seasoning and serve.

G. LEE'S BAKED HUSH PUPPIES

This is a variation on an old southern favorite that is usually fried. The recipe was originated by a Texas gentleman named G. Lee.

    1 cup yellow cornmeal
    1 cup flour
    3 teaspoons baking powder
    1 teaspoon salt
    1 teaspoon sugar
       Large pinch cayenne pepper
    ½ cup finely chopped onion
    1 large egg, beaten
    ⅓ cup milk
    2 tablespoons vegetable oil

1. Preheat oven to 425° F. Spray muffin tins with nonstick spray.

2. In a medium bowl blend cornmeal, flour, baking powder, salt, sugar, and cayenne. Stir in onion.

3. In a small bowl beat egg, milk, and oil. Add to cornmeal mixture and stir to blend; do not overmix.

4. Spoon batter into prepared muffin cups, filling cups one half to two thirds full. Bake until golden (15 to 20 minutes).

Makes about 12.

YANKEE DOODLE COLESLAW

This is a great make-ahead salad. It keeps very well, so make extra for leftovers.

    14 cups (2 large heads)
        shredded cabbage
     1 green bell pepper, chopped
     1 red bell pepper, chopped
     2 large white onions, minced
     1 cup vegetable oil
    1½ cups white vinegar, or to taste
    1½ cups sugar, or to taste
     1 tablespoon salt
     1 teaspoon celery seed

Combine cabbage, peppers, and onion in a large bowl. In a medium saucepan combine oil, vinegar, sugar, salt, and celery seed. Bring to a boil. Pour over cabbage mixture. Let stand without stirring for 1 hour. Then mix well and refrigerate. The slaw will keep several weeks and remain crisp.

Makes about 2 quarts.

This holiday barbecue ends with a non-traditional watermelon, made from rhubarb ice cream or raspberry sherbet with chocolate chips for seeds.

FROZEN WATERMELON BOMBE

This ice cream bombe looks like a watermelon. It's a visual treat as well as a taste treat and very appropriate for the Fourth of July. You may want to serve your bombe on a bed of cracked ice, just as you might chill and serve a real melon.

> 1 quart French Vanilla Ice Cream (see page 22), slightly softened
> ¼ cup miniature semisweet chocolate chips
> 1 quart Rhubarb Ice Cream (see page 70) or Raspberry Sherbet (see page 65), slightly softened
> Green food coloring

1. Place an 8-cup melon-shaped mold in the freezer for at least 1 hour.

2. Line inside of mold with an even layer of Vanilla Ice Cream. Cover with plastic wrap, pressing against the ice cream to seal it tightly and fill any air pockets. Return mold to freezer for at least 4 hours.

3. Stir chocolate chips into Rhubarb Ice Cream to simulate watermelon seeds; remove plastic wrap from mold and fill cavity with ice cream. Top with plastic wrap and freeze until firm.

4. To unmold, dip quickly in lukewarm water and invert onto a chilled platter. Return to freezer to set exterior.

5. Paint outside of molded ice cream with green food coloring, varying shades to resemble stripes on a real watermelon. Cover well and keep frozen. Slice to serve.

Serves 8 to 10.

RASPBERRY–WHITE CHOCOLATE TRUFFLE ICE CREAM

This sweet, trufflelike ice cream is studded with plump, tart berries.

> ½ cup sugar
> ½ cup water
> 4 large egg yolks, at room temperature
> 8 ounces white chocolate, melted and cooled
> 1 cup fresh raspberries, coarsely chopped
> 1 cup whipping cream

1. In a small saucepan over low heat, boil sugar and the water until sugar dissolves. Meanwhile, beat egg yolks in an electric mixer until they are pale yellow and a slowly dissolving ribbon forms when beaters are lifted. Beat in hot syrup in a thin, steady stream. Return to saucepan.

2. Stir over low heat until mixture thickens and a finger drawn across the spoon leaves a path (4 to 5 minutes). Do not boil, or mixture will curdle. Strain into a clean bowl and cool thoroughly.

3. Whisk chocolate into egg mixture. Fold in raspberries. Whip the cream to soft peaks and fold in. Transfer to an ice cream machine and freeze according to manufacturer's instructions.

Makes about 1 quart.

FROZEN BLACKBERRIES AND CREAM

This soft, heavenly concoction goes beautifully with fresh sliced peaches.

> 1 pint fresh blackberries
> 1 tablespoon lemon juice
> ½ to ⅔ cup superfine sugar
> 2 tablespoons wild blackberry liqueur or any other liqueur
> ½ cup whipping cream

1. Purée berries with lemon juice. Strain purée to make it perfectly smooth. Stir in sugar and liqueur.

2. Beat the cream to stiff peaks. Fold into purée, one third at a time. Pour into a 2-quart freezerproof glass bowl and freeze until firm.

Serves 8 to 10.

BLACK-VELVET ICE

This dessert offers a tart, refreshing combination of flavors.

> ¾ cup Guinness Stout, chilled
> ¾ cup extra-dry Champagne, chilled
> 1½ cups Simple Sugar Syrup, chilled (see page 15)
> 1 tablespoon lemon juice

Combine all ingredients. Transfer to an ice cream machine and freeze according to manufacturer's instructions.

Makes about 1½ pints.

FROZEN CHOCOLATE ESPRESSO

Don't let warm weather stop you from enjoying the luscious combination of coffee and chocolate.

> 3 ounces semisweet chocolate
> 3 tablespoons coffee-flavored liqueur
> 3 tablespoons water
> 6 large eggs, separated
> ¾ cup sugar
> 2 tablespoons instant espresso powder
> 1 teaspoon vanilla extract
> 1½ cups whipping cream
> 2 ounces bittersweet chocolate, grated
> 8 candied coffee beans, for garnish

1. In a small, heavy-bottomed saucepan over low heat, melt chocolate with liqueur and the water. Let cool slightly. In a medium bowl cream together egg yolks, sugar, espresso powder, and vanilla. Add melted chocolate and mix well.

2. Whip the cream to soft peaks. Fold into chocolate mixture.

3. Beat egg whites to stiff peaks; do not let them dry out. Fold in chocolate mixture. Pour into an 8-cup soufflé dish or 8 individual 1-cup ramekins. Sprinkle grated chocolate on top and garnish with a candied coffee bean. Freeze until firm (at least 4 hours).

Serves 8.

WATERMELON SHERBET

Any of your favorite melons can be substituted.

- ¼ cup sugar, or to taste
- ¼ teaspoon salt
- 1 heaping quart chilled watermelon chunks, seeds removed (about one 4-lb melon)
- 2 large egg whites

1. Sprinkle sugar and salt over melon chunks and mix well. Once sugar has dissolved, taste melon for sweetness; add more sugar if desired.

2. Purée melon, any juice it has released, and egg whites in a food processor or blender. Chill well. Transfer to an ice cream machine and freeze according to manufacturer's instructions.

Makes about 1 quart.

CHOCOLATE SHERBET

Chocolate lovers will welcome this light, refreshing dessert on those hot summer nights.

- ¾ cup unsweetened cocoa powder
- ½ cup sugar
  Pinch of salt
- 1¾ cups whole or low-fat milk
- 1½ teaspoons vanilla extract

1. In a medium saucepan combine cocoa, sugar, and salt; mix well. Gradually stir in milk. Bring just to a boil over moderate heat, stirring constantly. Reduce heat and simmer 5 minutes, still stirring.

2. Remove from heat and let cool. Add vanilla. Transfer to an ice cream machine and freeze according to manufacturer's instructions.

Makes about 1½ pints.

If you like to relax with coffee and cookies but have been yearning for something different, try curling up with Frozen Chocolate Espresso and homemade Kourabiedes (see page 50).

No one will ever guess how easy it is to assemble this sumptuous Strawberry Strata. A clear glass bowl is a must for showing off the jewel-like layers.

of moistened cake slices. Top with enough ice cream to cover cake completely; be sure ice cream reaches to edges of dish. Scatter some berries over ice cream, especially at edges. Continue layering with cake, ice cream, and berries, ending with a layer of ice cream topped with berries. (You should have 9 layers in all.) Cover well and freeze until firm.

3. In a small bowl whip the cream. Before serving cake, garnish with whipped cream rosettes and toasted almonds. Serve with Raspberry Purée.

Serves 10 to 12.

Coffee Strata Use Coffee Ice Cream (see page 22) in place of Strawberry, coffee-flavored liqueur in place of kirsch, and bits of crushed toffee candy in place of strawberries. Omit Raspberry Purée.

Dark Chocolate Strata Use Dark Chocolate Ice Cream (see page 39) in place of Strawberry, orange-flavored liqueur in place of kirsch, and raspberries in place of strawberries.

Peach Strata Use Peach Ice Cream (see Fresh Fruit Ice Cream, page 25) in place of Strawberry, amaretto in place of kirsch, and coasely chopped peaches in place of strawberries. Omit Raspberry Purée.

Banana Strata Use Banana Ice Cream (see Fresh Fruit Ice Cream, page 25) in place of Strawberry, dark rum in place of kirsch, and a combination of rum-soaked raisins and walnuts in place of strawberries. Omit Raspberry Purée.

Apricot Strata Use French Vanilla Ice-Cream (see page 22) in place of Strawberry, apricot brandy in place of kirsch, and coarsely chopped apricots in place of strawberries. Omit Raspberry Purée.

Pineapple Strata Use Burnt-Sugar Ice Cream (see page 25) in place of Strawberry, cognac in place of kirsch, and fresh pineapple chunks in place of strawberries. Omit Raspberry Purée.

STRAWBERRY STRATA

Strata means layers, in this case layers of tender pound cake, velvety ice cream, and icy berries.

- 1 Pound Cake (see page 102)
- ½ cup kirsch or any other liqueur
- 1 quart Strawberry Ice Cream (see page 22), softened
- 1 pint fresh strawberries, sliced or chopped
- ½ cup whipping cream
- ⅓ cup sliced almonds, toasted (see Rocky Road Ice Cream, Note, page 22)
- 1 recipe Raspberry Purée (see page 112)

1. Slice pound cake into ½-inch-thick pieces. Cut each piece diagonally to make 2 triangles. Brush both sides of each triangle with kirsch.

2. In a 3-quart or larger freezerproof clear glass dish, lay down a layer

FALL

With the shorter days and brilliant colors of fall come harvests of apples, grapes, pumpkins, and pears—inspiration for a new repertoire of frozen desserts. The lazy days of summer are gone, and countless activities return to full swing. Make-ahead desserts, ready in the freezer, mean more time for all the things you want to do.

QUICK APPLE SEMIFREDDO

The taste of applesauce comes through loud and clear in this easy-to-prepare dessert.

  1 cup applesauce
  2 large egg whites
  ¼ cup sugar
  ½ teaspoon vanilla extract
  ½ cup whipping cream

1. In a large mixing bowl, combine applesauce, egg whites, sugar, and vanilla. Beat until light and fluffy (2 to 4 minutes).

2. In a medium bowl whip the cream until stiff and fold into applesauce mixture. Spoon into small baking pan or metal bowl. Freeze until firm. Let stand at room temperature about 10 minutes before serving. Spoon into dessert dishes.

Serves 6.

FIG AND RUM ICE IN PAPAYA SHELLS

This dessert offers a glorious combination of flavors.

  1 cup sugar
  2 cups water
  12 plump fresh figs
  2 tablespoons rum
  1 tablespoon lemon juice
  3 ripe papayas, halved
    and seeded
    Fresh mint leaves, for garnish

1. In a medium saucepan boil sugar and the water together for 5 minutes. Cool completely.

2. Gently wash and trim figs. Purée in a blender or food processor. Chill purée well.

3. Mix together chilled fig purée, rum, lemon juice, and cooled sugar syrup. Transfer to an ice cream machine and freeze according to manufacturer's instructions. Spoon ice into papaya halves and garnish with fresh mint leaves.

Serves 6.

FROZEN PUMPKIN MOUSSE IN LACE SHELLS

Crisp, nutty cookie cups show off the delicate pumpkin mousse. Canned pumpkin works just as well as fresh in this dessert preparation. Don't make the shells when it's raining; they won't get crisp.

  ¾ cup water
  ¾ cup sugar
  3 large egg whites, at
    room temperature
    Pinch of salt
    Pinch of cream of tartar
  ½ cup pumpkin purée
  ¼ teaspoon each ground
    cinnamon, ground ginger,
    and ground nutmeg
  1 cup whipping cream
  2 tablespoons bourbon

Lace Shells

  ¼ cup unsalted butter, melted
  ¼ cup firmly packed
    dark brown sugar
  ¼ cup light corn syrup
  ½ cup flour
  ½ cup finely chopped walnuts
  2 teaspoons vanilla extract

1. In a small, heavy-bottomed saucepan, cook the water and sugar over low heat, stirring occasionally, until sugar dissolves. Increase heat and cook without stirring until syrup reaches soft-ball stage (238° F; see page 16).

2. Meanwhile, in the large bowl of an electric mixer, beat egg whites until foamy. Add salt and cream of tartar and beat to soft peaks. With the mixer running, add hot syrup in a thin, steady stream and continue beating until meringue is cool (about 10 minutes).

3. In a small bowl combine pumpkin, cinnamon, ginger, and nutmeg. Mix well. In a separate bowl whip the cream to soft peaks; fold in bourbon, and fold into pumpkin mixture. Fold into meringue. Freeze about 4 hours. (If freezing longer, let soften in refrigerator for 2 hours before serving.) Spoon mousse into Lace Shells and serve.

Makes about 1 quart.

Lace Shells

1. Preheat oven to 350° F. Melt butter in a small, heavy-bottomed saucepan. Add brown sugar and corn syrup. Bring to a boil over high heat, stirring constantly. Remove from heat. Add flour and walnuts all at once; stir until smooth. Blend in vanilla.

2. Drop mixture by teaspoonfuls about 3 inches apart on foil-covered baking sheets. Bake until cookies are a rich golden brown (7 to 10 minutes).

3. Remove cookies with a metal spatula and immediately drape them over inverted 2½-inch-diameter ramekins or custard cups (see illustration, page 50). Let cool, then store in an airtight container.

Makes about 2 dozen shells.

Step·by·Step

MAKING CHOCOLATE SHELLS

Scallop shells are a good size and shape for molding edible dessert dishes. You can substitute other large shells if you prefer. This technique can be used to make spectacular edible containers from such ordinary items as paper muffin cup liners, custard cups, and other small, decorative bowls.

1. *Cover the back of two 5-inch scallop shells with a layer of plastic wrap and then a layer of foil. Press the foil snugly against the shell to pick up the details of its ridges.*

2. *Lightly brush the foil with oil. Place the shells, foil side up, on a baking sheet.*

3. *Melt the chocolate in the top of a double boiler. Spoon about three quarters of the chocolate over the shells, smoothing it with a knife. Store in a cool place until hard (at least 2 hours).*

4. *Lift the chocolate with foil and plastic attached off the shells. Carefully pull the foil and plastic away from the chocolate, trimming the edges with a knife when necessary.*

5. *Reheat the remaining chocolate and use it to repair any cracks and to paint the inside of the chocolate shells. Store in a cool place until needed.*

FROZEN PERSIMMON CREAM IN CHOCOLATE SHELLS

The rich browns and oranges of fall come through in this lovely dessert. The delicate flavor of persimmon becomes stronger after the dessert has "ripened" in the freezer. Make the chocolate shells as described at left for individual servings or larger to serve two to four.

 4 *medium persimmons
   (2 cups pulp; see Note)*
 3 *tablespoons sugar*
 3 *tablespoons lemon juice*
 1 *tablespoon orange-
   flavored liqueur*
1½ *cups whipping cream, chilled*

Chocolate Shells

 1 *tablespoon vegetable oil*
 ½ *pound white or dark chocolate*

1. Cut persimmons in half and remove center membrane. Scoop out pulp with a spoon.

2. In a medium bowl combine pulp, sugar, lemon juice, and liqueur; mix well. In a separate bowl whip the cream to soft peaks. Fold in pulp mixture. Pour into a freezerproof bowl and freeze until firm. To serve, scoop into Chocolate Shells.

Serves 8.

Chocolate Shells Make 2 shells as illustrated at left. If you wish to make more than 2 shells, simply multiply the recipe.

Note . You can save whole ripe persimmons up to 6 months by freezing them. Let thaw 20 minutes at room temperature before cutting and scooping out pulp.

PUMPKIN ICE CREAM SQUARES

This is a perfect dessert for children's Halloween parties.

- 1½ cups graham cracker crumbs
- ¼ cup granulated sugar
- ¼ cup unsalted butter, melted
- 2 cups pumpkin purée
- ½ cup firmly packed dark brown sugar
- ½ teaspoon salt
- 1 teaspoon ground cinnamon
- ¼ teaspoon ground ginger
- ⅛ teaspoon ground cloves
- 1 quart French Vanilla Ice Cream (see page 22), softened
- ½ cup whipping cream (optional)
- 9 walnut halves (optional)

1. In a small bowl mix crumbs with granulated sugar and butter. Press into bottom of a 9-inch-square pan.

2. In a medium bowl combine pumpkin, brown sugar, salt, cinnamon, ginger, and cloves. Fold in softened ice cream. Spread in crumb-lined pan. Cover and freeze until firm. Cut into 3- by 3-inch squares. Whip the cream and decorate each square with whipped cream and walnut halves (if desired).

Makes 9 squares.

SPICED PEAR FROSTY

This spicy frozen drink can be prepared quickly for unexpected guests.

- 3 or 4 Bartlett pears, peeled and coarsely chopped (3 cups)
- 2 tablespoons lemon juice
- ½ cup milk
- ¼ teaspoon each ground nutmeg and ground cinnamon
  Sugar, to taste (optional)

1. In a large bowl toss pears with lemon juice. Spread in a single layer on a baking sheet. Freeze, uncovered, until solid.

2. Place frozen pears, milk, nutmeg, and cinnamon in a food processor or blender. Process until smooth. If the machine struggles to process frozen fruit, let fruit stand 10 minutes at room temperature to thaw slightly.

3. Add sugar to taste, if necessary. Serve in tall glasses with long-handled iced tea spoons.

Serves 4 to 6.

COUPE NORMANDE

This dessert is inspired by the classic combination of apples and cream traditional in the Normandy region of France.

- 4 tablespoons unsalted butter
- 4 apples, peeled, cored, and sliced
- ½ cup sugar
- ¼ cup calvados
- 1½ pints French Vanilla Ice Cream (see page 22)

1. In a heavy skillet melt butter and add apples. Cook over medium heat, stirring gently, 6 to 10 minutes. Cook apple slices so that they remain firm; do not let them become mushy.

2. Add sugar and cook 2 minutes more. Sprinkle with liqueur and ignite. When flames die out, serve apples over scoops of French Vanilla Ice Cream.

Serves 4 to 6.

LONITA'S COFFEE SORBET

There is no last-minute fuss when you serve this cup of espresso.

- ⅓ cup sugar, or to taste
- 3 tablespoons instant espresso powder
- 1 tablespoon coffee-flavored liqueur (optional)
- 2 cups boiling water
- 8 lemon twists (thin strips of lemon peel, about 2 in. long), for garnish
- 8 candied coffee beans, for garnish

Mix sugar with espresso powder and liqueur (if used). Add the boiling water and stir to dissolve. Refrigerate until thoroughly chilled. Transfer to an ice cream machine and freeze according to manufacturer's instructions. Serve in individual demitasse cups, each garnished with a lemon twist and a candied coffee bean.

Serves 8.

GRAPE SORBET WITH CHOCOLATE GRAPES

Experiment with different types of grape juice for a variety of interesting flavors.

- 1 cup Simple Sugar Syrup (see page 15), chilled
- 1 cup grape juice, chilled
- 2 tablespoons raspberry-flavored vinegar

Chocolate Grapes

- 8 ounces semisweet chocolate
- 1 bunch red or green seedless grapes
  Mint leaves, for garnish

Combine syrup, juice, and vinegar. Transfer to an ice cream machine and freeze according to manufacturer's instructions. Serve each scoop of sorbet with a decorative cluster of Chocolate Grapes.

Makes 1 pint.

Chocolate Grapes Melt chocolate in the top of a double boiler. Remove from heat. Rinse grapes and dry thoroughly. With a fork, dip one grape at a time into chocolate and place on a foil-lined baking sheet to dry. On a serving plate arrange chocolate-dipped grapes in clusters of 8 to 10; garnish each cluster with a sprig of mint to represent grape leaves. Store in refrigerator until ready to serve.

The king of cheeses becomes the queen of ice creams in a delightful presentation. The full flavor of Brie comes through in this ultra-creamy dessert.

BRIE ICE CREAM

This is an unusual ice cream served with dried apricots, figs, and candied walnuts. It is also excellent with fresh berries or topped with toasted pine nuts.

> 4 large egg yolks
> 8 ounces Brie, rind removed, at room temperature
> 1 cup sugar
> 1 cup whipping cream, chilled
>   Dried apricots, for accompaniment
>   Figs, for accompaniment

Candied Walnuts

> 1 cup sugar
> ½ cup water
> ½ teaspoon salt
> 1 teaspoon ground cinnamon
> 1½ teaspoons vanilla extract
> 2½ cups walnut halves

In a food processor or blender, combine egg yolks, Brie, sugar, and cream, and mix all the ingredients well. Transfer to an ice cream machine and freeze according to manufacturer's instructions. Serve with dried apricots, figs, and Candied Walnuts.

Makes about 1 pint.

Candied Walnuts In a medium saucepan cook sugar, the water, salt, and cinnamon to the soft-ball stage (238° F; see page 16) without stirring. Remove from heat; add vanilla and walnuts. Stir gently until nuts are well coated and mixture becomes creamy. Turn out onto waxed paper. Separate walnuts as they cool. Store in airtight container in a cool, dry place.

Makes about 2 dozen walnut halves.

AUTUMN HARVEST FESTIVAL SUPPER

Chilled Acorn Squash and Pear Soup

Torta Rustica

Oil-cured olives, garnished with fresh herb sprigs

Pasta al Pesto Salad

Applejack Ice Cream With Spicy Apple Compote

Suggested beverage: Chardonnay or sparkling apple juice

As the earthy colors of fall replace the gleaming greens of summer, appetites revived by cooler weather long for heartier fare. Even if you don't spend your days working in the fields, you can celebrate autumn's bounty with a hearty harvest supper. The first-of-autumn combination of acorn squash and pears offers a fitting welcome to the new season. A satisfying Torta Rustica combines beauty with make-ahead ease. To finish the meal, autumn's quintessential fruit, the apple, is highlighted twice in a simultaneously hot and cold dessert.

CHILLED ACORN SQUASH AND PEAR SOUP

This unlikely combination is sure to please.

- ¼ teaspoon ground mace
- 2 cinnamon sticks
- 2 bay leaves
- 1½ teaspoons black peppercorns
- 2 pounds acorn squash, peeled, seeded, and cut into large cubes
- 3 large ripe pears, halved and cored
- 1 cup yellow onion, coarsely chopped
- 1 teaspoon kosher salt
- 3 cups unsweetened apple juice
- 3½ cups chicken stock
  Juice of 2 large lemons
- ⅓ cup acorn squash, blanched and cut into 1- by ¼-inch strips, for garnish
- ⅓ cup pears, cut into 1- by ¼-inch strips, for garnish
- 2 tablespoons black walnut pieces, for garnish

1. Tie mace, cinnamon, bay leaves, and peppercorns in a piece of cheesecloth.

2. In a large pot combine squash cubes, pear halves, onion, salt, apple juice, stock, and lemon juice. Bring to a boil; skim liquid. Add cheesecloth-wrapped spices and simmer, partially covered, 45 minutes.

3. Remove from heat and let cool until lukewarm. Strain liquid and reserve. Discard cheesecloth-wrapped spices. In a blender or food processor, purée cooked pear and squash until smooth. Combine liquid with purée. Strain through a fine mesh strainer and let cool. Refrigerate until well chilled. Serve in chilled bowls, garnished with squash and pear strips and walnut pieces.

Serves 6.

TORTA RUSTICA

This is a meal in itself, ideal for picnics.

- 1 package dry yeast
- ¼ cup warm water
- 1½ teaspoons sugar
- 6 tablespoons unsalted butter, softened
- 2 large eggs
- 2 cups flour
- ½ teaspoon salt
- 1 medium onion, chopped
- ½ pound mushrooms, sliced
- 1 tablespoon whipping cream
- 1 large egg yolk
- 2 cups diced cooked ham
- ½ pound sliced provolone cheese
- 1 jar (7 oz) roasted red peppers, cut into thin strips
- 1 package (10 oz) frozen artichoke hearts, thawed, drained, and chopped

1. Dissolve yeast in the warm water, then add sugar. Add 4 tablespoons softened butter, eggs, flour, and salt; beat well. Cover and refrigerate 4 to 24 hours. Dough will be sticky.

2. Preheat oven to 375° F. Grease an 8-inch springform pan. In a medium sauté pan, melt remaining 2 tablespoons butter. Sauté onion and mushrooms until tender. Drain.

3. On a floured board roll out ⅔ of the dough into a 13- to 14-inch circle. Press evenly into prepared pan, covering bottom and sides. Beat cream and egg yolk together to make a glaze; brush lightly over dough (reserve remaining glaze for step 5).

4. Fill pan in layers in the following order: the ham; half of the cheese; the mushrooms and onions; the remaining cheese; the pepper strips; and the artichoke hearts.

5. Roll remaining dough into an 8-inch circle; brush with reserved glaze. Place dough glazed side down over filling. Press edges together to seal, and tuck them under. Slash center for a steam vent. Brush top with glaze. Bake 35 minutes. Loosen torta from pan with a flexible spatula. Cut into wedges and serve warm or at room temperature.

Serves 8.

Applejack Ice Cream With Spicy Apple Compote is a fitting finale for a colorful autumn meal. Choose from the myriad apple varieties available in your area.

PASTA AL PESTO SALAD

The incomparable taste of fresh basil makes this simple salad a winner.

> 1 pound rotelle or similar pasta
> 2 cups fresh basil leaves, lightly packed
> 3 cloves garlic, peeled and minced
> ¼ cup freshly grated Parmesan cheese
> 1 tablespoon pine nuts
> ¾ cup olive oil
> 2 teaspoons salt, or to taste
> 3 tablespoons chopped sun-dried tomatoes (optional)

1. Cook pasta in a very large pot of boiling water. When pasta is al dente (fully cooked but still lightly firm), drain and rinse with cold water to cool (see Note).

2. In a food processor or blender, purée basil, garlic, cheese, pine nuts, oil, and salt. Toss with pasta. Taste for seasoning; add more salt, pepper, or oil if necessary. Top with tomatoes (if desired).

Serves 4 to 6.

Note Step 1 can be completed 2 days in advance if you store drained pasta in an airtight container in the refrigerator. Before proceeding with recipe, place pasta in a colander and rinse again with cold water to prevent sticking.

APPLEJACK ICE CREAM WITH SPICY APPLE COMPOTE

The warm compote, pungent with spices and tart fall apples, is served over creamy Applejack Ice Cream.

> 1 recipe French Vanilla Ice Cream (see page 22)
> ¼ cup applejack

Spicy Apple Compote

> 4 tablespoons unsalted butter
> 2 pounds tart apples, peeled, cored, and coarsely chopped
> ½ cup sugar
> ¼ cup applejack
> ¼ teaspoon each ground cinnamon and ground allspice
> ¼ cup golden raisins

Prepare French Vanilla Ice Cream as directed, adding applejack to finished ice cream base.

Makes 1 quart.

Spicy Apple Compote Melt butter in a heavy skillet over medium heat. Add apples and sugar and cook until apples caramelize and become soft. Add applejack, cinnamon, allspice, and raisins. Reduce heat to medium-low and cook 2 to 3 minutes more. Spoon over ice cream and serve immediately.

Makes 2 cups.

FRESH APPLE SORBET

The flavor of this sorbet will vary with the variety of apple you choose.

> 6 tart green apples, peeled
> 1 cup Simple Sugar Syrup (see page 15)
> 1 tablespoon lemon juice

Chop apples in a food processor or blender with syrup and lemon juice until slightly chunky; do not make completely smooth. Transfer to an ice cream machine and freeze according to manufacturer's instructions.

Makes 1 quart.

APPLESAUCE SORBET

With simple syrup in the refrigerator and applesauce on the shelf, you are always ready for unexpected guests.

> 3 cups unsweetened applesauce
> 1 cup Simple Sugar Syrup (see page 15)
> 1 tablespoon ground cinnamon

Combine all ingredients. Transfer to an ice cream machine and freeze according to manufacturer's instructions.

Makes 1 quart.

JUICY FRUIT SHERBET

Here's a way to turn too-ripe bananas into a richly flavorful dessert. Store very ripe bananas in their skins in the freezer. The skin will turn black, but the fruit inside will retain its natural color. Use them straight from the freezer.

> 2 cups Simple Sugar Syrup (see page 15)
> ¾ cup lemon juice
> 1½ cups orange juice
> 3 very ripe bananas, peeled and mashed
> 1 teaspoon lemon zest, finely chopped
> 1 tablespoon orange zest, finely chopped
> 1 cup whipping cream, chilled
> 3 large egg whites, at room temperature
> Pinch cream of tartar

1. In a large bowl combine simple syrup, lemon juice, orange juice, mashed bananas, lemon zest, and orange zest. Chill.

2. In a medium bowl whip the cream to soft peaks. In another bowl beat egg whites and cream of tartar to soft peaks (see page 14).

3. Fold whipped cream into fruit mixture, then fold in egg whites. Transfer to an ice cream machine and freeze according to manufacturer's instructions.

Makes 2 quarts.

WINTER

As the year comes to an end, we all quicken our pace in anticipation of the holiday season. No other time of year evokes such strong memories of past celebrations or such high emotions. With winter upon us, who does not think of such traditional delights as mincemeat and cranberries, eggnog and plum pudding? Frozen desserts, made well before company arrives, allow you to enjoy the deeply satisfying flavors of the season and still have time to spend with friends and family.

FROZEN PUMPKIN PIE

Surprise your guests with a frozen version of everyone's holiday favorite.

> 1 can (1 lb) pumpkin
> ¾ cup firmly packed
>   dark brown sugar
> ⅓ cup granulated sugar
> 1 egg plus 1 yolk, large
> 1 cup milk
> 1 cup whipping cream
> ½ teaspoon salt
> 1 teaspoon ground cinnamon
> ½ teaspoon ground ginger
> ¼ teaspoon each ground cloves
>   and ground nutmeg
> 1 teaspoon vanilla extract

Walnut Pie Shell

> 2½ cups finely chopped walnuts
> ½ cup unsalted butter, softened
> 2 tablespoons brandy
> ⅓ cup firmly packed
>   dark brown sugar

1. Have Walnut Pie Shell ready in freezer.

2. Combine all ingredients in a large bowl and mix well. Transfer to an ice cream machine and begin to freeze according to manufacturer's instructions. When ice cream is almost frozen, transfer it to Walnut Pie Shell. Smooth top. Cover with plastic wrap and freeze until firm (about 4 hours).

Serves 8 to 10.

Walnut Pie Shell Combine all ingredients in a bowl. Press into a 10-inch glass pie plate, covering bottom and sides. Freeze until needed.

SWEDISH SORBET

This dessert is popular in Sweden, a country known for its berries and its aquavit.

> 1 bag (12 oz) cranberries
> 1 cup water
> ¾ cup sugar
> ½ cup orange juice
> 3 tablespoons lemon juice
>   Zest of 1 lemon, finely chopped
> ½ cup milk
> ½ cup aquavit

1. In a medium saucepan bring cranberries, the water, sugar, orange juice, lemon juice, and lemon zest to a boil. Cook about 10 minutes, stirring occasionally, until berries have popped and mixture is thick. Remove from heat and let cool.

2. In a food processor or blender, purée mixture until it is liquid. Add milk and aquavit; mix well.

3. Transfer to an ice cream machine and freeze according to manufacturer's instructions.

Makes 1 quart.

MAPLE MOUSSE

Try dressing up this rich mousse by sprinkling chopped toasted walnuts over the top.

> 4 large egg yolks
> ½ cup pure maple syrup
> ¾ cup whipping cream
> 1 tablespoon vanilla extract
>   or Canadian whiskey

In an electric mixer beat egg yolks and maple syrup until very thick and pale. Mixture will triple in volume. In a separate bowl whip the cream. Fold whipped cream and vanilla into egg-syrup mixture. Freeze in a 1-quart soufflé dish.

Serves 8.

PLUM PUDDING ICE CREAM

Ice cream lovers will welcome this untraditional approach to an old English holiday favorite.

> 3 cups whipping cream
> 1 cup milk
> 1 cup sugar
> 4 large egg yolks
> 2 teaspoons vanilla extract
> ¼ cup port
> ½ cup golden raisins
> 1 can (16½ oz) purple plums,
>   drained, pitted, and
>   coarsely chopped
> 1 teaspoon ground ginger
> ½ cup chopped walnuts
> 6 gingersnaps, crumbled
>   (about ½ cup)

1. In a heavy-bottomed 2-quart saucepan, heat cream, milk, and sugar, stirring occasionally, until sugar is dissolved and mixture is hot but not boiling.

2. Whisk egg yolks in a bowl. Keep whisking and very slowly pour in 1 cup of the hot cream mixture. When smooth, pour back into pan and cook over medium heat, whisking constantly, until mixture thickens slightly and coats the back of a spoon (about 5 minutes). Be careful not to boil mixture; it will curdle. Strain into a clean bowl and cool thoroughly. Add vanilla.

3. In a small saucepan heat port. Add raisins and simmer until all but 2 teaspoonfuls of port has evaporated. Let cool.

4. Transfer cooled egg-cream mixture to an ice cream machine and begin to freeze according to manufacturer's instructions. Near end of freezing process, remove ice cream from machine and fold in cooled raisin-port mixture, plums, ginger, walnuts, and gingersnaps.

5. Line a 6-cup mold with plastic wrap. Pour in ice cream and freeze until firm. When ready to serve, invert on a platter and carefully remove plastic wrap.

Serves 10 to 12.

CRANBERRY SORBET

This is ideal for a formal Christmas dinner party. Serve it in hollowed-out frozen lemon or orange shells, garnished with mint leaves.

> 1 cup cranberries
> 1 cup unsweetened
>   cranberry juice
> 1 cup water
> 1 cup sugar

1. In a medium saucepan cook cranberries, cranberry juice, and the water over medium heat until berries pop open and mixture thickens. Remove from heat, cool, and push through a sieve or food mill with a medium blade.

2. Add enough water to mixture to make 3 cups. Return to saucepan, add sugar, and cook over low heat until sugar is dissolved. Cool.

3. Transfer to an ice cream machine and freeze according to manufacturer's instructions.

Makes about 1½ pints.

MINCEMEAT ICE CREAM PIE

This will delight lovers of mincemeat pie à la mode.

> 1½ quarts French Vanilla Ice
>   Cream (see page 22), slightly
>   softened
> 1½ cups mincemeat
>   ½ cup chopped nuts, any kind
>   1 graham cracker crust (11
>   in.), baked 5 minutes
>   1 cup whipping cream
>   2 tablespoons brandy

1. In a large bowl combine ice cream, mincemeat, and nuts; mix well. Spread in crust and freeze until firm.

2. Whip the cream to soft peaks; fold in brandy. Spoon over pie and serve.

Serves 8 to 10.

CHAMPAGNE SORBET

Serve this easy and elegant dessert in crystal glasses.

> 3 cups Champagne
> ¼ cup sugar, or to taste

Mix Champagne and sugar. Transfer to a shallow pan and freeze until granular, stirring occasionally. Process in a blender or food processor for a few seconds to lighten sorbet. Refreeze until serving time.

Makes 3½ cups.

Mincemeat Ice Cream Pie, a frozen twist on an old family favorite, can be made far in advance to save the harried holiday hostess those precious moments.

menu

APRÈS-SKI DINNER

Endive With Curried Crab

Steak au Poivre

Oven-Roasted Potatoes

Purée of Parsnips

Frozen Bourbon Cream

*Suggested beverage: Pinot Noir
or ginger beer or warm cider*

*This hearty menu for four
will conquer appetites
built up on the slopes. Make
the Frozen Bourbon Cream
before you venture forth
in the morning. After a day
of skiing, the rest of the
menu can be assembled with
a minimum of effort. The
quickly made Endive With
Curried Crab can be enjoyed
while preparing the potatoes
and parsnip purée. Then
open the wine and enjoy a
glass as you prepare the
Steak au Poivre.*

*Whether you spend the day
skiing the mountains or reading
a book by the fire, this hearty
winter meal will warm you
body and spirit.*

ENDIVE WITH CURRIED CRAB

The sweetness of crab and the crunch of water chestnuts are perfect foils for the slightly bitter, tender leaves of Belgian endive.

- *1 cup crabmeat*
- *¼ cup mayonnaise*
- *2 teaspoons curry powder*
- *2 tablespoons chopped water chestnuts*
  Freshly ground white pepper, to taste
- *2 to 4 heads Belgian endive (amount depends on size of heads)*

1. In a small bowl combine crab, mayonnaise, curry powder, water chestnuts, and pepper.

2. Cut root end from endive so that leaves separate. Place 1 heaping teaspoon of crab mixture on root end of each leaf. Arrange filled endive leaves on a platter like spokes of a wheel and serve.

Makes 12 to 18 pieces.

STEAK AU POIVRE (PEPPER STEAK)

It is essential to crack the peppercorns just before using so they retain all their fragrant and volatile oils.

- *4 shell or rib-eye steaks (6 to 8 oz each), boned and trimmed*
- *1 teaspoon salt*
- *3 to 4 tablespoons freshly cracked black peppercorns*
- *4 tablespoons unsalted butter*
- *4 large shallots, peeled and minced*
- *2 tablespoons Cognac or brandy*
- *⅓ cup dry red wine*
- *3 tablespoons whipping cream*
- *1½ cups brown beef gravy, homemade or purchased*

1. Sprinkle both sides of each steak with salt. Spread crushed pepper on work surface and press both sides of each steak into it.

2. Heat butter in a large, heavy-bottomed skillet. When butter is a rich brown color, sauté steaks 3 to 5 minutes on each side, or until medium rare. Remove from pan and keep warm.

3. Add shallots to pan and sauté 1 minute. Add Cognac and ignite. When flames die out, add wine and bring to a boil. Reduce by half. Add cream and gravy and bring to another boil. Correct seasoning and pour over steaks.

Serves 4.

PURÉE OF PARSNIPS

This often overlooked root vegetable makes a delicious substitute for mashed potatoes.

- *1 pound parsnips, peeled and chopped into 1-inch pieces*
- *2 cups water*
- *1 tablespoon unsalted butter*
- *2 tablespoons whipping cream Salt and freshly ground pepper, to taste*

In a medium saucepan boil parsnips in the water until easily pierced with a knife (about 10 minutes). Drain and purée through a food mill or food processor. Stir in butter and cream. Season to taste with salt and pepper.

Serves 4.

FROZEN BOURBON CREAM

The flavor will vary with your choice of bourbon; each type of bourbon has its own distinctive taste.

- *1 cup sugar*
- *1 cup water*
- *8 large egg yolks*
- *⅓ cup bourbon*
- *1 cup whipping cream*

1. In a small saucepan boil sugar and the water over high heat until sugar dissolves. Continue boiling, without stirring, for 5 minutes. Meanwhile, in the large bowl of an electric mixer, beat egg yolks at high speed for 2 minutes. Reduce speed to medium and, with mixer running, add hot sugar syrup to yolks in a thin stream. When mixture begins to thicken, increase speed to high. Continue beating until thick and completely cool (about 20 minutes). Fold in bourbon.

2. Whip cream to soft peaks. Fold into yolk mixture. Divide among 8 wineglasses, cover glasses with plastic wrap, and freeze.

Serves 8.

FROZEN EGGNOG

Since this mixture does not freeze solid, you can bring it directly from the freezer to the table. Serve it in punch cups.

- *8 large egg yolks*
- *1 cup sugar*
- *1 cup dark rum*
- *½ cup brandy*
- *2 teaspoons vanilla extract*
- *6 cups whipping cream, well chilled*

1. In the large bowl of an electric mixer, whip egg yolks. Gradually add sugar and continue to beat until mixture is thick and light yellow. Gradually beat in rum, brandy, and vanilla; this will make the mixture liquid again. Set aside.

2. In a separate bowl whip cream to soft peaks. Whisk about one third of the cream into egg yolk mixture until thoroughly incorporated. Then fold in remaining cream and pour into a 3-quart punch bowl. Cover tightly with plastic wrap and freeze. To serve, spoon into punch cups or dessert dishes.

Serves 12.

PRUNE AND ARMAGNAC ICE CREAM

This is a favorite in southwestern France. The Brandied Prunes must be stored four to six months to develop their full flavor before they are used. They are well worth waiting for, for use in this unusual ice cream or simply spooned with their sauce over vanilla ice cream.

- 1 cup sugar
- 2 cups milk
- 2 cups whipping cream
- 10 large egg yolks
- 2 teaspoons vanilla extract
- 2 tablespoons liquid from Brandied Prunes

Brandied Prunes

- 1 pound grade AA California prunes (preserved without sulfur dioxide)
- 2 cups Armagnac

1. In a heavy-bottomed 2-quart saucepan, heat sugar, milk, and cream. Stir occasionally until sugar is dissolved and mixture is hot but not boiling.

2. Whisk egg yolks in a bowl. Continue whisking and pour in 1 cup of the cream mixture in a thin, steady stream. When smooth, pour back into pan of hot liquid. Cook, whisking constantly, until mixture thickens slightly and coats the back of a spoon (about 5 minutes). Be careful not to let mixture boil, or it will curdle. Strain into a clean bowl and cool thoroughly. Add vanilla.

3. Chop 1½ cups of the Brandied Prunes. Add chopped prunes and the 2 tablespoons liquid from Brandied Prunes to egg-cream mixture. Transfer to an ice cream machine and freeze according to manufacturer's instructions.

Makes about 1 quart.

Brandied Prunes Place prunes in a glass container with a tight-fitting lid. Pour in Armagnac. Seal and store 4 to 6 months before using.

Makes about 1½ pints.

FROZEN FRUITCAKE

This dessert is a helpful addition to the busy host's pantry during the holiday season.

- 2 cups milk
- ½ cup sugar
- ¼ cup flour
  Pinch of salt
- 2 large eggs, beaten
- 2 teaspoons vanilla extract
- 1 cup dried currants
- 2 cups macaroon crumbs
- ½ cup mixed candied fruit
- 1 cup chopped nuts, any kind
- 1 cup whipping cream
  Chopped nuts, for garnish (optional)

1. In a medium saucepan over medium heat, stir together milk, sugar, flour, and salt. Cook, stirring constantly, until mixture is smooth and starts to thicken (about 5 minutes). Add eggs and cook, stirring, until thick (3 to 5 minutes). Remove from heat and stir in vanilla. Cool.

2. Stir in currants, crumbs, candied fruit, and nuts. In a separate bowl whip the cream. Fold in whipped cream and pour into a greased and waxed paper–lined 4½- by 8½- by 2½-inch loaf pan. Wrap and freeze. Slice frozen and serve, garnished with chopped nuts (if desired).

Serves 8.

WINTER-FRUIT COMPOTE

Try this combination of favorite winter fruits and spices over Burnt-Sugar Ice Cream (see page 25).

- 2 cups apple juice
- 2 cinnamon sticks
- 2 whole cloves
- 2 tart apples, peeled, cored, and chopped
- 2 ripe pears, peeled, cored, and chopped
- ½ cup fresh orange juice
- 2 navel oranges, peeled and sectioned, membrane removed
- 1 cup seedless green grapes

In a medium saucepan combine apple juice, cinnamon sticks, cloves, apples, and pears. Simmer over medium heat, stirring occasionally, for 15 minutes. Let mixture cool slightly, then add orange juice, oranges, and grapes. Remove cloves and cinnamon sticks. Serve fruit warm over ice cream. Compote may be stored chilled for up to 1 week.

Makes 1 quart.

BOURBON ICE CREAM WITH CHOCOLATE-BOURBON SAUCE

This double-bourbon treat features the world's two favorite flavors: vanilla and chocolate.

- 6 large egg yolks
- 1 cup sugar
- 2 cups milk
- ⅓ cup bourbon
- 1½ tablespoons vanilla extract
- 2 cups whipping cream

Chocolate-Bourbon Sauce

- 1 pound semisweet chocolate, chopped
- ½ cup unsalted butter
- ½ cup milk
- ½ cup whipping cream
- ¼ cup bourbon

1. In the large bowl of an electric mixer beat egg yolks and sugar until mixture is thick and forms a ribbon when beaters are lifted. In a medium saucepan over medium heat, combine yolk mixture and milk. Simmer, stirring constantly, until mixture is thick and coats the back of a spoon (about 5 minutes).

2. Remove from heat, add bourbon and vanilla, and let cool. Whip the cream to very soft peaks; blend into bourbon mixture. Transfer to an ice cream machine and freeze according to manufacturer's instructions.

Makes about 1 quart.

Chocolate-Bourbon Sauce In a heavy-bottomed saucepan over low heat, melt chocolate and butter. Add milk and cream, stirring over heat until mixture is smooth. Add bourbon and remove from heat. Serve warm over ice cream.

Makes about 2 cups.

The sweet-tart flavor of kumquats makes an unusual and lively ice. For an especially festive presentation, serve garnished with candied kumquats.

FRESH KUMQUAT ICE

Golden, sweet-sour kumquats have a short season; be sure to take advantage of their unique flavor while they're available.

>   2 cups fresh kumquats
>   1¼ cups sugar
>   2 cups water
>   1½ cups orange juice
>   3 tablespoons lemon juice

1. Halve kumquats and purée in a food processor or blender. Transfer to a medium saucepan. Add sugar and bring to a boil over medium heat. Reduce heat and simmer 15 minutes, stirring frequently.

2. Remove from heat and add the water, orange juice, and lemon juice. Strain into a clean bowl and cool thoroughly.

3. Transfer to an ice cream machine and freeze according to manufacturer's instructions.

Makes about 1 quart.

CANDIED KUMQUATS

Candied kumquats look like small lotus blossoms. Serve them with ice cream or with Fresh Kumquat Ice (see preceding recipe).

>   1 pound (about 30)
>   fresh kumquats
>   2½ cups sugar
>   ¾ cup water

1. Remove small stem ends from kumquats. Make 4 evenly spaced lengthwise slits around each fruit. Place in a medium saucepan and cover with water. Lightly poach over medium heat 5 to 7 minutes, then drain well. Do not overcook kumquats, or they will fall apart during the next step.

2. To make crystallized kumquats, in the same pan combine 1½ cups of the sugar and the water. Stir well, add drained kumquats, and bring to a slow boil. Cook uncovered over low heat about 30 minutes, watching to make sure sugar doesn't caramelize. If sugar starts to brown, lower heat.

3. Drain crystallized kumquats on a wire rack for 10 minutes, making sure they don't touch each other. Put remaining sugar in a bowl and roll each kumquat in sugar. Allow kumquats to dry overnight on a wire rack. Transfer to small paper candy cups to prevent fruit from sticking together and store in an airtight container.

Makes about 30 kumquats.

CHESTNUT ICE CREAM

This very rich ice cream is wonderful served with a snifter of brandy and roasted chestnuts, fresh from the fire.

>   ¾ cup milk
>   ¾ cup whipping cream
>   1 cup sugar
>   4 large egg yolks
>   1 can (8¾ oz) crème de
>   marrons (chestnut spread)
>   2 teaspoons vanilla extract
>   2 tablespoons dry sherry
>   1 tablespoon brandy or rum

1. In a medium saucepan heat milk, cream, and sugar, stirring occasionally, until sugar is dissolved and mixture is hot but not boiling.

2. Whisk egg yolks together in a bowl. Continue whisking and very slowly pour in 1 cup of the cream mixture. When smooth, pour back into pan. Whisk constantly over low heat until mixture coats the back of a spoon (see Basics, step 3 and photograph, page 13).

3. Strain into a clean bowl and add chestnut spread, vanilla, sherry, and brandy. Transfer to an ice cream machine and freeze according to manufacturer's instructions.

Makes about 1½ pints.

COUPE MARRON

This is a perfect ending for Christmas dinner. Chestnut pieces in vanilla syrup come in cans from France and Italy; look for them on the shelves of specialty-food stores.

>   1½ pints French Vanilla Ice
>   Cream (see page 22)
>   1 cup chestnut pieces in
>   vanilla-flavored syrup
>   ½ cup whipping cream
>   3 tablespoons chopped bitter-
>   sweet or semisweet chocolate

Scoop ice cream into 6 large wine glasses. Spoon chestnuts and their syrup over top. Whip the cream. Garnish coupe with whipped cream and chopped chocolate.

Serves 6.

ORANGE SHERBET

To serve in an unusual and attractive way, pipe the sherbet through a pastry bag into chilled glass dishes or champagne glasses and refreeze until serving time.

>   Zest of 1 orange
>   4 cups fresh orange juice
>   2¾ cups sugar
>   2 cups water
>   Juice of 1 lemon

1. Place zest in a fine strainer and pour boiling water over it. Drain.

2. In a medium saucepan over high heat, bring orange juice, sugar, the water, and lemon juice to a boil, stirring occasionally. Boil for 5 minutes. Remove from heat and let cool. Add orange zest.

3. Transfer to an ice cream machine and freeze according to manufacturer's instructions.

Makes about 1 quart.

Select your favorite type of pear to star in a chocolate extravaganza, the justly famous Poires Belle Hélène (see page 115).

Frozen Desserts

Frozen desserts are a favorite of people the world over. They come in a wide variety of shapes—cakes, pies, tortes, bombes, even logs. Whatever shape they take, they are sure to please. A big reason for the popularity of frozen desserts is that they make life easier for the busy host or hostess. Made ahead, they remove some of the hustle and bustle that surround entertaining. From a quick and easy Frozen Peanut Cream (see page 111) to a sophisticated Grand Marnier Soufflé (see page 103) to surprising Cinnamon Tostadas With Warm Apple Purée and Chocolate-Cinnamon Sauce (see page 105), frozen desserts fit the diversity of today's tastes and the demands of our fast-paced life-style.

CAKES

Just about everyone likes cake with ice cream. For most of us, that traditional combination is the focal point of every birthday party and many other celebrations and has been for as long as we can remember. The basic sponge cake recipes that follow will produce light and elegant cakes, perfect partners for your favorite ice creams. Match them with various toppings (see pages 27 to 33) for an unlimited repertoire of ice cream tortes. For more adventurous desserts combine your cake and ice cream in unusual ways—in cake rolls (see page 101), a trifle (see page 102), or a meringue and ice cream cake (see page 100).

BUTTER SPONGE CAKE (GÉNOISE)

This simple sponge cake is the foundation of many classic and contemporary desserts.

- 4 *large eggs, at*
  room temperature
- ⅔ *cup sugar*
- 3 *tablespoons unsalted*
  butter, melted
- ¾ *cup flour*

1. Preheat oven to 350° F. Grease and flour an 8-inch-diameter cake pan and line the bottom with parchment paper.

2. In a large bowl combine eggs and sugar and break up yolks with a whisk. Set bowl in a larger bowl containing hot, not boiling, water and beat eggs and sugar with a hand-held electric mixer until warm, frothy, and pale yellow.

3. Remove bowl from water and continue beating at high speed until batter has cooled, tripled in volume, and resembles softly whipped cream. Mix about ¼ cup of the egg mixture into melted butter. (This "lightens" butter, making it easier to incorporate into batter.)

4. Fold flour into egg mixture in 3 stages, folding gently but quickly. Just before final folding, add lightened butter and fold it in.

5. Turn into prepared baking pan and bake until cake shrinks slightly from edges of pan and top springs back firmly when depressed with your finger (20 to 30 minutes). Turn out of pan and cool right side up on a wire rack.

Serves 10.

Chocolate Butter Sponge Cake (Génoise) Reduce flour to ½ cup and combine with ¼ cup sifted unsweetened cocoa before folding in.

LINDA COLLINGS'S BERRY SHORTCAKE

Fresh berries and berry ice cream top this rich and flavorful shortcake.

- 3½ *cups flour*
- ½ *cup granulated sugar*
- 1½ *teaspoons salt*
- 1½ *tablespoons*
  baking powder
  Zest of 1 lemon,
  finely chopped
- 6 *tablespoons unsalted butter,*
  cold
- 2 *cups whipping cream*
- 4 *tablespoons*
  granulated sugar
- 2 *pints fresh berries, such as*
  strawberries, blackberries,
  blueberries, raspberries,
  or a combination
- 2 *tablespoons firmly packed*
  dark brown sugar
- 1 *pint Fresh Berry Ice Cream*
  (see Fresh Fruit Ice Cream,
  page 25), for topping

1. Preheat oven to 350° F. In a large bowl combine flour, the ½ cup granulated sugar, salt, and baking powder; mix well. Add lemon zest. Cut in butter until mixture looks like large peas. Transfer 2½ cups of the mixture to a separate bowl. Set the rest aside.

2. To the 2½ cups mixture, add 1 cup of the cream and mix to a soft dough. Be careful not to overmix. On a floured board roll dough into an 11-inch-diameter circle. Line a 9-inch pie pan with it; trim the edges.

3. In a medium bowl combine the 4 tablespoons granulated sugar and berries. Toss until berries are coated. Fill pie shell with berries.

4. Add remaining cream to the reserved flour-butter mixture; mix to a paste. With your floured fingers cover berries with paste. Sprinkle brown sugar over the top and bake until firm and slightly browned on top (40 to 50 minutes). Let cool slightly and serve in wedges topped with a scoop of Fresh Berry Ice Cream.

Serves 8 to 10.

PUMPKIN LOAF TORTE

Chocolate chips in pumpkin? Try this for a flavorful combination.

- 1¾ *cups flour*
- 1 *teaspoon baking soda*
- 1 *teaspoon ground cinnamon*
- ½ *teaspoon salt*
- ½ *teaspoon ground nutmeg*
- ¼ *teaspoon each ground ginger*
  and ground cloves
- ½ *cup unsalted butter, at*
  room temperature
- 1 *cup sugar*
- 2 *large eggs*
- ¾ *cup pumpkin purée*
- ¾ *cup chocolate chips*
- ¾ *cup chopped walnuts*
- 1 *pint Chocolate Chip Ice Cream*
  (see page 22), slightly softened

1. Preheat oven to 350° F. Grease and flour a 9- by 5-inch loaf pan.

2. In a medium bowl combine flour, baking soda, cinnamon, salt, nutmeg, ginger, and cloves.

3. In a large bowl cream butter and sugar together until light and fluffy. Add eggs and mix well. Add pumpkin, then flour mixture. Mix well. Stir in chocolate chips and ½ cup of the nuts. Pour into prepared loaf pan. Sprinkle with remaining nuts. Bake until firm to the touch in center (about 1 hour and 10 minutes).

4. Remove cake from pan and cool completely on a wire rack. Slice horizontally into thirds. Spread half the ice cream on the bottom layer. Add the middle layer and spread with remaining ice cream. Add top layer. Wrap tightly and freeze until firm. Serve in 1-inch-thick slices.

Serves 8 to 10.

ASSEMBLING AN
ICE CREAM TORTE

1. Slice a Butter Sponge Cake or Chocolate Butter Sponge Cake (see page 98) in half horizontally with a long-bladed serrated knife.

2. If desired, lightly brush each cut layer with Simple Sugar Syrup (see page 15) flavored with any liqueur of your choice.

3. Spread a pint of softened ice cream evenly over the bottom layer.

4. Lay the second layer on top, pressing down all over the cake to make it even. Wrap tightly in plastic wrap and freeze.

5. Remove cake from freezer about 10 minutes before serving. Drizzle a topping over the torte and pass the remainder in a gravy boat.

Invent Your Own Tortes

Create distinctive tortes by combining your favorite ice cream flavors and toppings with a basic Butter Sponge Cake. Here are some suggested combinations.

Combine Vanilla Butter Sponge Cake with:

Rocky Road Ice Cream (page 22) and Fresh Cherry Sauce (page 42)

Chocolate Ice Cream (page 22) and Chocolate-Rum Sauce (page 28)

Chocolate Chip Ice Cream (page 22) and Chocolate-Raspberry Sauce (page 28)

Combine Chocolate Butter Sponge Cake with:

Peppermint-Stick Ice Cream (page 23) and Peppermint Sauce (page 39)

Peanut Butter Ice Cream (page 25) and Jam Sauce (page 33)

Maple-Walnut Ice Cream (page 23) and Maple Sauce (page 28)

*Let the good times roll.
Create your own ice cream
cake rolls featuring your
favorite ice creams and
sauces. Here blueberry ice
cream (see Fresh Fruit Ice
Cream, page 25) is
wrapped in a buttery
Vanilla Sponge Cake and
topped with spicy
Cinnamon-Blueberry
Sauce (see page 28).*

MERINGUE–ICE CREAM CAKE

The crunchy meringue is a wonderful
contrast to the smooth ice cream.

  1 *cup confectioners' sugar*
  6 *tablespoons unsweetened
     cocoa powder*
  6 *large egg whites, at
     room temperature*
  ¼ *teaspoon cream of tartar*
  ¾ *cup plus 2 teaspoons
     granulated sugar*
  1 *quart ice cream, any flavor*
  ¾ *cup whipping cream,
     well chilled*
  1 *recipe sauce of choice
     (see pages 27 to 33)*

1. Preheat oven to 180° F. Draw a
9-inch-diameter circle on each of
2 sheets of parchment paper. Turn
each sheet over onto a baking sheet;
butter the paper and very lightly dust
it with flour. Fit a pastry bag with
a ½-inch plain tip.

2. Sift confectioners' sugar with
cocoa. In an electric mixer at medium speed beat egg whites and
cream of tartar until soft peaks form.
Add ¾ cup of the granulated sugar a
tablespoon at a time and beat until
meringue is shiny. Gently fold in
cocoa mixture.

3. Place meringue in pastry bag; pipe it out in a spiral about ¾ inch thick beginning at the middle of one of the drawn circles and spiraling outward until the circle is completely covered. Repeat for the second circle, then bake until the meringues are firm (1 to 1½ hours). Remove meringues and attached paper from pans and set on oven rack. Continue baking for another hour. The meringues will be firm and dry to the touch. Gently release them from the paper with a large metal spatula. If the bottom of a meringue is sticky, return it to the pan and bake until dry. Cool on a rack.

4. Trim meringue layers to fit inside a 9-inch springform pan. Set 1 meringue in pan. Spread with half of the ice cream. Place second meringue on top. Spread with remaining ice cream. Wrap tightly and freeze overnight (see Note).

5. Just before serving the cake, whip the cream with the remaining 2 teaspoons granulated sugar until soft peaks form. Run a knife around the edge of the pan to release the sides and then remove cake from pan. Spread whipped cream in a thin layer over the top and sides of the cake. Drizzle sauce over the cake. Slice and serve immediately.

Serves 10 to 12.

Note Meringues may be made ahead and stored in an airtight container.

ICE CREAM CAKE ROLL

A gala rolled cake with a pinwheel interior is the pride and joy of many an ice cream shop. A little advance planning makes this spiral treat a snap to make at home. Use the combinations of ingredients suggested in the Tips box at right or let inspiration guide you in creating your own signature dessert.

1 quart ice cream, any flavor
1 recipe topping (see pages 25 to 33), any flavor, or 1½ cups sliced fresh fruit, for garnish

Vanilla Sponge Cake

⅔ *cup confectioners' sugar*
6 *eggs, separated, plus 2 egg whites, extra large*
½ *teaspoon vanilla extract*
¾ *cup flour*
Confectioners' sugar, for sprinkling towel

1. Prepare Vanilla Sponge Cake.

2. Let ice cream soften at room temperature for 10 to 15 minutes before using. It must be just soft enough to spread.

3. Unroll cooled cake onto tea towel it was rolled with; spread ice cream evenly over cake surface. Re-roll cake, lifting towel to help with rolling and keep cake tight. Work gently to prevent tearing. Wrap completed roll in plastic wrap and freeze.

4. To serve, let roll stand at room temperature for 10 minutes. Garnish with topping or sliced fresh fruit. Slice with a serrated knife.

Serves 8 to 10.

Vanilla Sponge Cake

1. Preheat oven to 350 °F. Butter and flour a 9- by 13-inch jelly-roll pan, then line it with parchment paper.

2. Set aside 2 tablespoons of the sugar. In a medium bowl beat remaining sugar with egg yolks until mixture doubles in bulk and becomes light and fluffy. Mix in vanilla.

3. In another bowl beat 8 egg whites to soft peaks. Add reserved sugar and continue beating until stiff. Fold yolk mixture carefully into whites, then quickly but gently fold in flour.

4. Spread batter evenly in prepared pan. Bake until cake is golden brown and springs back when touched (8 to 10 minutes). Meanwhile, sprinkle a tea towel with confectioners' sugar. When cake is done, immediately turn pan over towel and let cake fall out. Peel parchment off cake, then roll cake in towel, jelly-roll style, and let cool completely.

Makes one 9- by 13-inch cake.

Chocolate Sponge Cake Substitute ¼ cup unsweetened cocoa for ½ cup of the flour.

Tips

... FOR CREATING SPECTACULAR ICE CREAM CAKE ROLLS

Any kind of ice cream can be used in an ice cream cake roll. For the best visual result, use a colorful ice cream with vanilla cake and a light-colored ice cream with chocolate cake. Serve with a sauce of either a complementary or a contrasting flavor. The following suggested combinations will get you started.

☐ Vanilla Sponge Cake with Dark Chocolate Ice Cream (page 39) and Chocolate-Raspberry Sauce (page 28)

☐ Vanilla Sponge Cake with Burnt-Sugar Ice Cream (page 25) and Spiced Peach Sauce (page 30)

☐ Vanilla Sponge Cake with Fresh Blueberry Ice Cream (Fresh Fruit Ice Cream, page 25) and Cinnamon-Blueberry Sauce (page 28)

☐ Chocolate Sponge Cake with Peppermint-Stick Ice Cream (page 23) and Marshmallow Sauce (page 30)

☐ Chocolate Sponge Cake with White Chocolate Ice Cream (page 40) and Miss Jane Marble Sauce (page 31)

☐ Chocolate Sponge Cake with Coconut Ice Cream (page 35) and Chutney Vanilla Sauce (page 31)

☐ Chocolate Sponge Cake with Peanut Butter Ice Cream (page 25) and Almond-Raisin Fudge Sauce (page 27)

FROZEN DESSERTS FROM AROUND THE WORLD

Frozen desserts are favorite treats all over the world. Italians love Tortoni (see page 106) and Spumoni (see page 107); the French love Profiteroles (see page 106) and Fromage Blanc Pastries (see page 109). Nearly every country has its own special favorites. The following recipes capture some of the distinctive flavors of a number of countries in a selection of traditional and not-so-traditional international desserts.

MADELEINE–ICE CREAM MOLD

The tender little cakes in Marcel Proust's description of a perfect tea also go perfectly with ice cream. To vary the effect, try using Chocolate Madelines (see page 47) with a complementary ice cream flavor.

> 3 large eggs
> ½ cup granulated sugar
> ½ cup unsalted butter, melted and cooled
> 1 cup sifted flour
> ½ teaspoon baking powder
> 1 teaspoon vanilla extract
> Confectioners' sugar, for dusting
> 1 recipe Simple Sugar Syrup (see page 15), flavored with liqueur, if desired
> 1 quart ice cream, any flavor, softened

1. Preheat oven to 375° F. Generously grease 2 madeleine pans (24 little cakes).

2. In a medium bowl beat eggs until foamy. Add granulated sugar gradually, beating until thick, pale, and double in volume. Stir 1 heaping tablespoon of egg mixture into butter.

3. Gently fold flour and baking powder into remaining egg mixture. Add vanilla and melted butter mixture, folding only until mixed. Fill molds three fourths full with batter. Bake only until cake springs back when pressed in the center (8 to 10 minutes). Remove from molds and sprinkle tops with confectioners' sugar. Cool.

4. To assemble mold: Oil a 5-cup ring mold; place in freezer until well chilled. Line mold with madeleines, rounded sides down, edges touching. You should use 16 to 18 madeleines. Brush with syrup. Spread half of the softened ice cream over madeleines, pressing down gently to fill in the spaces around them.

5. Crumble remaining madeleines and sprinkle over ice cream. Spread remaining ice cream in the mold, pressing down and smoothing the top. Wrap tightly and freeze.

6. To serve: Run a knife around the outer and inner edges of the mold to loosen the dessert. Dip the mold in room-temperature tap water for 5 seconds; pat dry. Shake the mold downward once over a platter to release the dessert. Slice and serve.

Serves 6 to 8.

FROZEN YOGURT TRIFLE

As long as you have a pound cake on hand, you can put together this British dessert in minutes.

> 1 package (10 oz) frozen raspberries in light syrup, partially thawed
> 1 package (10 oz) frozen strawberries in light syrup, partially thawed
> 2 cups low-fat plain yogurt
> ⅓ cup sugar
> 2 tablespoons kirsch

Pound Cake

> ½ pound unsalted butter, softened
> 1 cup plus 2 tablespoons sugar
> 4 large eggs, at room temperature
> ½ teaspoon vanilla extract
> 1⅔ cups flour

1. In a food processor or blender, purée raspberries and strawberries in their syrup. Strain through a fine-meshed sieve to remove seeds. Return to processor and add yogurt, sugar, and kirsch. Mix until smooth.

2. Spoon yogurt mixture into a shallow baking pan and freeze until firm. Slice half of the Pound Cake into ⅓-inch-thick slices (reserve the other half of the cake for another use). Make a layer of cake slices in a large glass trifle dish or glass bowl. Turn out the frozen yogurt mixture and cut it into ⅓-inch-thick slices. Place a layer of frozen yogurt slices on top of the pound cake.

3. Continue layering cake and frozen yogurt slices until both are used up; end with a layer of frozen yogurt slices on top.

Serves 12.

Pound Cake

1. Preheat oven to 325° F. Butter a 5-cup loaf pan.

2. In a medium bowl cream butter and sugar together with an electric mixer until light and fluffy. Add eggs one at a time, beating well after each addition. Don't worry if batter looks curdled. Add vanilla, then fold in flour, mixing well. Pour batter into prepared loaf pan.

3. Place loaf pan on a baking sheet and bake until top of cake is light brown and firm to the touch (50 or 60 minutes). A skewer inserted into the center should come out clean. Cool the cake right side up on a wire rack to room temperature.

Makes 1 pound cake.

TRIPLE-CHOCOLATE BAVAROISE

This fabulous, rich dessert was inspired by French cooking teacher and cookbook author Madeleine Kamman. It is equally delicious frozen or thawed in the refrigerator.

> 1⅓ cups whipping cream, chilled
> ¼ cup B&B liqueur
> 1 tablespoon vanilla extract
> 4 large egg yolks
> 1 cup milk
> 1½ tablespoons unflavored gelatin
> 6 ounces white chocolate, chopped
> 2 ounces unsweetened chocolate, chopped
> Pinch of salt
> 3 ounces semisweet chocolate, chopped

1. Whip the cream to light Chantilly stage (see page 14), then fold in liqueur and vanilla. Refrigerate until needed (step 3).

2. Mix egg yolks and milk. Cook in a medium saucepan over moderate heat, stirring constantly, until mixture begins to thicken. When hot, add a few tablespoons of mixture to gelatin to melt it. Add white chocolate and unsweetened chocolate to mixture; stir until chocolate melts. Add salt and melted gelatin. Mix well.

3. Place saucepan over a bowl of ice and stir until mixture begins to thicken again. Remove from ice; stir in prepared cream and semisweet chocolate. Turn into a freezerproof bowl and freeze until firm.

Serves 8 to 10.

FROZEN GRAND MARNIER SOUFFLÉ

This is a variation on a French classic.

    6 large egg yolks
    ¾ cup sugar
    3 cups whipping cream
    3 tablespoons Grand Marnier
       liqueur
    1 tablespoon finely chopped
       orange zest

1. In a medium bowl beat egg yolks and sugar together until thick and pale yellow.

2. In a separate bowl whip the cream to soft peaks. Fold liqueur and orange zest, then cream into egg mixture.

3. Pour into a 1-quart soufflé dish fitted with a collar (see Frozen Lemon Soufflé, page 70, step 1) or into individual soufflé dishes. Freeze at least 4 hours.

Serves 6 to 8.

Never worry about a sinking soufflé again. This never-fail Frozen Grand Marnier Soufflé guarantees a taste sensation, and a carefree host.

Discover the depth of cinnamon's distinctive flavor, as set off by applesauce and chocolate, in dessert tostadas inspired by tastes from south of the border.

CINNAMON TOSTADAS WITH WARM APPLE PURÉE AND CHOCOLATE-CINNAMON SAUCE

Try this for a cool and crunchy ending to your next Mexican meal.

Apple Purée

3 pounds apples, peeled and cored
½ cup unsalted butter
1 cup sugar
3 tablespoons lemon juice
½ teaspoon ground cinnamon
¼ teaspoon freshly grated nutmeg
2 tablespoons Calvados or applejack

Cinnamon Tortillas

1 tablespoon ground cinnamon
4 tablespoons sugar
  Vegetable oil, for frying
8 flour tortillas, (4 in. each, cut from 8-in. tortillas, if necessary)

Cinnamon Ice Cream

1 recipe French Vanilla Ice Cream (see page 22)
3 tablespoons ground cinnamon

Mexican Chocolate Ice Cream

3 ounces Mexican chocolate (see Note)
1 ounce unsweetened chocolate
1 recipe French Vanilla Ice Cream Base I (see page 13)

Chocolate-Cinnamon Sauce

4 ounces semisweet chocolate, finely chopped
1 cup water
¼ cup sugar
½ cup whipping cream
¼ teaspoon ground cinnamon
2 tablespoons Mexican coffee-flavored liqueur (optional)

To assemble: Warm the Apple Purée. Spoon about ½ cup of the Apple Purée on 1 side of each dessert plate. Place a warm tortilla on the other side of the plate. Place 2 scoops of ice cream—cinnamon, chocolate, or one of each—on top of the tortilla and drizzle about 3 tablespoons of sauce on top. Serve immediately.

Serves 8.

Apple Purée

Place all ingredients in a 2½-quart saucepan. Cover and cook over medium heat, stirring occasionally, until apples are soft (about 25 minutes). Purée in a food processor or blender.

Makes about 1 quart.

Make-Ahead Tip Purée may be kept in the refrigerator several days; before using, reheat.

Cinnamon Tortillas

1. In a small bowl combine cinnamon and sugar; set aside.

2. In a large skillet heat about ½ inch of oil over medium-high heat. Fry tortillas, turning once, until they are golden (about 1 minute). Transfer tortillas to paper towels to drain. Sprinkle with cinnamon-sugar mixture.

Makes 8 tortillas.

Cinnamon Ice Cream
Make French Vanilla Ice Cream as directed, adding cinnamon at same time as the sugar for the custard.

Makes about 1 quart.

Mexican Chocolate Ice Cream

1. Slowly melt the chocolates together in a double boiler. Meanwhile, prepare the French Vanilla Ice Cream Base.

2. Slowly add ½ cup of the warm ice cream base to the melted chocolate, whisking constantly to keep chocolate smooth. Return mixture to ice cream base, mix well, and let cool.

3. Transfer to an ice cream machine and freeze according to manufacturer's instructions.

Makes about 1 quart.

Note If Mexican chocolate is unavailable, use semisweet chocolate and add 1 teaspoon ground cinnamon and ½ teaspoon vanilla extract to the French Vanilla Ice Cream Base.

Chocolate-Cinnamon Sauce

1. Combine chocolate, the water, and sugar in a heavy-bottomed 1-quart saucepan. Gradually bring to a boil, stirring constantly. When the chocolate has melted, stir in cream and cinnamon.

2. Strain mixture into a small bowl and add liqueur (if used). Serve immediately or cover and refrigerate until needed. Rewarm over low heat.

Makes about 1¾ cups.

MEXICAN ZABAGLIONE

This interpretation of a traditional Italian dessert is made with Mexican coffee-flavored liqueur instead of Marsala wine and is served frozen instead of hot.

8 large egg yolks
½ cup sugar
1 cup Mexican coffee-flavored liqueur

In a medium saucepan beat egg yolks until pale yellow. Add sugar and continue beating until thick. Gradually add liqueur, beating constantly. Place pan over medium heat and continue to beat constantly until mixture foams and begins to thicken. Transfer to a freezerproof glass bowl and freeze for at least 4 hours.

Serves 4 to 6.

MEXICAN FRIED ICE CREAM

This will surprise you with its hot, crispy coating and cool interior.

1 pint French Vanilla Ice Cream (see page 22)
½ cup crushed cornflakes or vanilla wafer crumbs
1 teaspoon ground cinnamon
2 teaspoons sugar
1 large egg
Vegetable oil, for deep-frying
Honey, for garnish
Whipped cream, for garnish

1. Scoop out balls of ice cream measuring about 1½ inches in diameter. Freeze until firm.

2. In a medium bowl combine cornflakes, cinnamon, and sugar. Divide mixture in half. Roll frozen ice cream balls in half the mixture and freeze again.

3. Beat egg. Dip coated balls into beaten egg. Roll again in crumbs and freeze. (For a thicker coating, remove from freezer, roll a third time in egg and crumbs, and refreeze.)

4. When ready to serve, heat oil to 350° F. Place 1 or 2 frozen balls in a slotted spoon and lower into the hot oil. Cook 1 minute and remove immediately. Drizzle with honey and top with whipped cream.

Serves 4.

FROZEN PROFITEROLES

A classic French pastry dough is the basis for a wonderful frozen dessert.

1 cup water
½ cup unsalted butter, at room temperature, cut into 8 equal pieces
1 tablespoon sugar
Pinch of salt
1 cup flour
5 large eggs, 1 mixed with 1 tablespoon whipping cream, for glaze (optional)
1 quart French Vanilla Ice Cream (see page 22)
2 cups Old-Fashioned Chocolate Sauce (see page 30)

1. Preheat oven to 400° F. Place oven rack in center position.

2. In a medium saucepan over moderately high heat, stir the water, butter, sugar, and salt together with a wooden spoon. When butter has melted and the water has come to a full boil, remove from heat and immediately add all the flour.

3. Stir vigorously until mixture forms a ball. Using the wooden spoon or an electric mixer, thoroughly beat in 4 of the eggs, one at a time. Continue to beat for another minute, until egg mixture is smooth and shiny.

4. Using a spoon or a pastry bag fitted with a large tip, drop generous teaspoonfuls of the egg mixture about 2 inches apart onto 2 parchment-lined baking sheets. Brush with egg glaze, if desired.

5. Bake for 15 minutes, then reduce temperature to 350° F and bake for an additional 30 minutes. Remove puffs from the oven and cut a small slit in each with a sharp knife so that steam will escape and they will remain crisp.

6. When puffs are cool cut off the upper third of each with a serrated knife. Use your fingers to remove the soft dough inside. Generously fill the cavity of each puff with ice cream. Replace the "lids" on top of the ice cream. Freeze immediately.

7. To serve, spoon about ¼ cup of the chocolate sauce onto each dessert plate and top with 3 profiteroles.

Serves 8.

TORTONI

Your guests will never guess how simple this Italian treat is to prepare.

1 cup whipping cream
¼ cup confectioners' sugar
½ cup crushed Amaretti cookies or chopped, toasted almonds (see Rocky Road Ice Cream, Note, page 22)
3 tablespoons amaretto
1 large egg white, at room temperature
Crushed Amaretti cookies, toasted almonds, or maraschino cherries, for garnish (optional)

1. In a medium bowl whip the cream and sugar to soft peaks. Fold in crushed cookies and amaretto. In a separate bowl beat egg white until stiff but still shiny and moist. Fold into whipped cream mixture.

2. Spoon into a 1-quart bowl, parfait glasses, or paper-lined muffin cups. Garnish (if desired). Cover tightly and freeze at least 6 hours.

Serves 8.

FROZEN CAMPARI-LEMON SOUFFLÉ

Here is a delicious way to use up egg whites left over from making ice cream. The tart flavor of Campari apéritif, an Italian favorite, makes this dessert unforgettable.

¾ cup plus 3 tablespoons sugar
½ cup water
3 large egg whites, at room temperature
Pinch of salt
Pinch of cream of tartar
¼ cup Campari
Zest of 1 lemon, very finely chopped
1 cup whipping cream, well chilled
Chopped almonds and whipped cream, for garnish (optional)

1. In a small, heavy-bottomed saucepan over low heat, heat ¾ cup of the sugar and the water until sugar dissolves. Boil until syrup reaches soft-ball stage (238° F on a candy thermometer, see page 16).

2. Using an electric mixer beat egg whites with salt and cream of tartar until just stiff, not dry. Beat in remaining sugar, 1 tablespoon at a time.

3. With the mixer running, slowly pour the boiling syrup into egg white mixture; continue to beat until cool. Beat in Campari and lemon zest.

4. In a separate bowl whip the cream to soft peaks. Fold one third of the cream into the Campari mixture to lighten it, then fold in the remaining whipped cream. Spoon into six 5- or 6-ounce individual soufflé dishes or a 1-quart soufflé dish. Freeze 4 to 24 hours. Garnish (if desired).

Serves 6.

ZUCCOTTO

Although one food critic compared eating this dessert to "something like eating a prom dress," your friends can't help but be impressed with this flamboyant Italian concoction.

> ¼ cup Cognac or rum
> 3 tablespoons cherry or amaretto liqueur
> 3 tablespoons orange-flavored liqueur
> 6 ounces semisweet chocolate, finely chopped
> 1 Pound Cake (see Frozen Yogurt Trifle, page 102)
> 3 cups whipping cream, chilled
> 1 cup confectioners' sugar
> 2 ounces hazelnuts, toasted, skinned, and chopped
> 2 ounces slivered almonds, toasted

1. Mix Cognac, cherry liqueur, and orange-flavored liqueur together. Reserve half the mixture and pour remainder into the top of a double boiler. Add 3 ounces of the chocolate and heat over simmering water until chocolate melts. Set aside.

2. Line a 3- or 4-quart round-bottomed bowl with plastic wrap or damp cheesecloth. Cut cake into ½-inch-thick slices, then cut each slice in half diagonally, making 2 triangles. Moisten triangles with reserved liqueur mixture. Completely line the bowl with the cake triangles,

narrowest points down. Make sure each crust side of a triangle lines up against the crustless side of the triangle next to it to produce a sunburst pattern when the cake is unmolded. Fill in any gaps with small pieces of moistened cake.

3. In a chilled bowl whip the cream and sugar to stiff peaks. Fold in hazelnuts, almonds, and remaining chocolate. Divide mixture in half. Spread one half evenly inside the cake-lined bowl. Blend the liqueur-chocolate mixture into the other half and use it to fill the cake's cavity.

4. Even off the surface, cutting away any protruding pieces of cake. Use the remaining pieces of liqueur-moistened cake to seal the top of the bowl. Cover tightly with plastic wrap and freeze for 24 hours.

5. To serve, cover the bowl with a flat serving dish and turn it upside down. Lift off the bowl and carefully remove the plastic wrap or cheesecloth. Cut into slices.

Serves 10 to 12.

SPUMONI

Myriad flavors dance a tarantella on your tongue.

> 2 cups whipping cream
> ¼ cup toasted almonds, chopped
> ¼ cup finely chopped maraschino cherries
> 2 tablespoons finely chopped candied citron
> Zest of 1 orange, finely chopped
> 2 ounces semisweet chocolate, finely chopped
> 3 tablespoons orange-flavored liqueur
> ¼ teaspoon almond extract
> ¾ cup sugar
> 4 tablespoons light corn syrup
> 6 large eggs, at room temperature

1. Oil a 6-cup ice cream mold. In a medium bowl whip the cream to stiff peaks. Fold in almonds, cherries, citron, orange zest, chocolate, liqueur, and almond extract. Set aside in the refrigerator.

2. In a small saucepan combine sugar and corn syrup. Heat to just below soft-ball stage (220° F on a candy thermometer).

3. Meanwhile, beat eggs until thick and pale yellow. Slowly pour sugar syrup into eggs, beating constantly. When all the syrup has been incorporated, place the bowl over ice and continue to beat until mixture is cool.

4. Fold one third of the whipped cream into mixture to lighten it, then fold in the rest. Pour into prepared mold and freeze for at least 6 hours.

Makes about 1½ pints.

PARMESAN ICE CREAM

This makes a wonderful companion to crisp apples, pears, grapes, or other fruits normally served with Parmesan cheese. Be sure to try it on top of a slice of warm apple pie.

> 2 cups whipping cream
> ⅔ cup fresh Parmesan cheese, finely grated
> 2 tablespoons sugar
> 1 tablespoon sweet paprika
> ⅛ teaspoon white pepper
> Fresh fruits, such as apples, pears, or grapes, for garnish

1. In a 1-quart saucepan, warm cream until it just reaches a simmer. Remove from heat.

2. Add cheese, sugar, paprika, and pepper to the pan and stir for a minute or so until most of the cheese dissolves. Pour into a bowl and chill at least 4 hours. Transfer to an ice cream machine and freeze according to manufacturer's instructions.

3. Line a 6-inch-diameter cake pan or other mold with plastic wrap. Pour in the frozen Parmesan cream, cover with another sheet of plastic wrap, and freeze for 4 or more hours.

4. To serve, remove the top layer of plastic wrap and invert the pan onto a chilled marble cheese board or chilled plate. Lift off the pan and peel off the plastic wrap to reveal the "wheel of cheese." Garnish with fresh fruits. Slice into wedges or shave off pieces with a cheese plane.

Serves 8 to 10.

Even if you're not Italian, you can dream of the beauty of Sicily as you enjoy this luxurious cassata laden with sweetmeats.

FABULOUS FREDDO

This is an Italian version of a frozen English trifle.

- 1 cup sugar
- ⅓ cup chopped hazelnuts
- 4 large egg yolks
- 3 tablespoons water
- 1 cup whipping cream
- 5 tablespoons dark rum
- 1 ounce semisweet chocolate, chopped
- 1 Butter Sponge Cake (see page 98), baked in an 8-inch-square pan

1. Make a praline by combining ½ cup sugar and hazelnuts in a small, heavy-bottomed saucepan. Cook over medium heat, stirring constantly, until sugar turns amber. Pour the praline onto a buttered sheet of aluminum foil and let cool. In a food processor fitted with a steel blade or in a blender, process the praline until powdery, leaving a few larger pieces for texture. Set aside. The praline may be made weeks ahead and stored in an airtight container.

2. To make a rum custard, in a medium bowl beat egg yolks until lemon colored. In a small, heavy-bottomed saucepan, bring remaining sugar and the water to a boil. Cook to soft-ball stage (238° F on a candy thermometer, see page 16). Beat hot syrup into yolks in a slow stream; continue beating until mixture is completely cool. Chill 15 to 20 minutes. Meanwhile, whip the cream to soft peaks. Fold whipped cream, 2 tablespoons rum, chocolate, and praline into mixture.

3. To assemble: Cut a section of sponge cake to fit a 3½- by 10-inch loaf pan. Place in pan. (Reserve remaining cake for another use.) Sprinkle cake with remaining 3 tablespoons rum. Top with rum custard. Wrap tightly and freeze overnight. To serve, unmold onto a platter and cut into slices.

Serves 8 to 10.

SICILIAN CASSATA

Cassata can be either fruit-filled ice cream, as it is here, or a rich layer cake with ricotta cheese, fruit, chocolate, and cream.

- 3 tablespoons dark rum or amaretto
- 1 tablespoon orange-flavored liqueur
- ¾ cup mixed candied fruit, chopped
- ¾ cup whipping cream
- 1 quart French Vanilla Ice Cream (see page 22), slightly softened
- ½ cup pistachio nuts, chopped
- ½ cup coarsely chopped semisweet chocolate
  Whipped cream, candied cherries, and cocoa powder, for garnish (optional)

1. Combine rum, liqueur, and candied fruit in a small bowl; set aside for at least half an hour.

2. Meanwhile, line a 2-quart loaf pan or mold with a large piece of plastic wrap, pressing it well into the corners. In a medium bowl whip the cream to soft peaks.

3. Spoon softened ice cream into a large bowl; fold in rum-fruit mixture, pistachio nuts, and chocolate. Gently fold in whipped cream.

4. Pour into plastic-lined pan. Tap the pan against a cutting board several times to fill the corners. Cover with plastic wrap and freeze overnight.

5. To serve, invert the pan on a chilled platter. Lift off the pan and remove the plastic wrap. Garnish cassata with whipped cream rosettes, candied cherries, or a light dusting of cocoa (if desired). Cut into slices.

Serves 8 to 10.

SWEETENED FROMAGE BLANC PASTRIES

Fromage blanc is a fresh goat cheese, popular in France and now also being made in America. If you can't find fromage blanc, you can substitute cream cheese.

- 6 sheets filo pastry
  Hazelnut oil, for brushing

Fromage Blanc Filling

- 8 ounces fromage blanc or cream cheese
- 2 ounces other soft goat cheese
- 2 large eggs
- ¼ cup whipping cream
- ¼ cup sugar
- 1 tablespoon finely chopped orange zest
- 1 tablespoon framboise (raspberry eau-de-vie)
- 2 tablespoons toasted hazelnuts, chopped (see Rocky Road Ice Cream, Note, page 22)

1. Preheat oven to 350° F. Brush each filo pastry sheet with oil and stack the sheets. Trim the stack into a 12- by 15-inch rectangle. Cut the rectangle into twenty 3-inch squares. Cut off the tips of the corners to help make them look round (they don't need to be perfectly round). Brush small, gem-sized cupcake tins with hazelnut oil. Press each dough square into a cup. If you wish, the cups can be chilled at this point and the recipe continued later.

2. Pour Fromage Blanc Filling into formed cups. Bake until cups are golden and filling is lightly puffed. Let cool completely on wire racks, then freeze. Thaw at room temperature for 10 minutes before serving.

Makes 20 to 26 pastries.

Fromage Blanc Filling Combine all ingredients and mix well.

Very special occasions call for Champagne. For a dramatic presentation, garnish pale Champagne Cream with berries and edible flowers such as borage (above) or nasturtiums.

CHAMPAGNE CREAM

The berries in this sparkling French dessert can be scattered over the finished custard, as instructed, or folded into the soft cream before freezing.

> 1½ cups whipping cream, chilled
> 2½ tablespoons sugar
> 8 large egg yolks
> ⅔ cup Champagne
> 1 pint fresh berries, any kind, for garnish

1. In a medium bowl whip the cream to soft peaks. Add ½ tablespoon of the sugar and continue whipping to stiff peaks.

2. Place egg yolks, remaining sugar, and Champagne in a heavy-bottomed saucepan or copper bowl. Sprinkle with a little cold tap water and cook over low heat, beating vigorously, until thick and creamy. Set pan over ice and let cool thoroughly.

3. Blend whipped cream into custard. Pour into a freezerproof bowl and freeze at least 6 hours. To serve, scatter berries over the top and serve from the bowl.

Serves 6.

CONFECTIONS

Some desserts are meant to melt in your hands as well as in your mouth. These toothsome morsels are easy to prepare, so they're sure to be as popular with you as with your guests.

FROZEN PEANUT CREAM

Here is a quick and easy peanut delight for adult tastes.

> 2 cups whipping cream
> 2 tablespoons dark rum
> ½ pound peanut brittle, crushed

1. In a large, chilled bowl whip the cream to soft peaks. Fold in rum and all but 3 tablespoons of the peanut brittle.

2. Pour mixture into small dessert bowls and freeze at least 1 hour. Garnish with reserved peanut brittle.

Serves 6 to 8.

PEPPERMINT-FUDGE CUPS

Once these confections are frozen, you can remove them from the muffin tins and store them in plastic bags in the freezer.

> 1 cup unsalted butter, at room temperature
> 2 cups confectioners' sugar
> 4 large eggs
> 4 ounces unsweetened chocolate, melted
> 2 teaspoons vanilla extract
> 1 teaspoon peppermint extract

1. With an electric mixer cream butter and sugar together at high speed for about 5 minutes. Beat in eggs, one at a time, making sure that each egg is completely incorporated before adding the next.

2. Beat in melted chocolate and continue to beat for another 2 minutes. Add vanilla and peppermint extracts.

3. Spoon into gem-sized muffin tins lined with paper candy cups. Freeze at least 2 hours.

Makes about 36.

CHOCOLATE SYRUP CREAM

Homemade chocolate syrup makes this an extraspecial treat, when you have the time to make it. When you don't, storebought syrup makes the recipe a breeze.

> 2 cups whipping cream, chilled
> 1⅓ cups Sweet Chocolate Syrup (see page 27) or Bittersweet Chocolate Syrup (see page 26)
> 3 tablespoons orange-flavored liqueur or dark rum
> 2 ounces semisweet chocolate, at room temperature, for garnish (optional)

1. In a large, chilled bowl whip the cream to soft peaks.

2. In a medium bowl fold about ¼ of the whipped cream into the chocolate syrup. Thoroughly fold chocolate mixture and liqueur into rest of whipped cream.

3. Pour mixture into a 1-quart freezerproof serving bowl or individual dessert bowls. With a vegetable peeler shave chocolate into curls for garnish, if desired, by drawing the peeler against the long edge of the piece of chocolate. (The chocolate must be warm to make curls; if it is cool you will get splinters.) Freeze entire dessert at least 4 hours.

Serves 6 to 8.

THE ULTIMATE PEPPERMINT STICK

Two favorite flavors make a fine combination: The sharpness of the peppermint is fresh and cooling against the smooth richness of the chocolate.

> 1 recipe Peppermint-Stick Ice Cream (see page 23)
> 1 package (8½ oz) chocolate wafer cookies
> 2 ounces peppermint-stick candies or candy canes, finely chopped
> 1 recipe Chocolate-Peppermint Topping (see page 33); optional

1. Spoon ice cream onto the center of an 18-inch-long piece of heavy-duty aluminum foil. Lift the short ends of the foil to meet in the center, loosely covering the ice cream. With your hands press against the foil and form the ice cream into a cylinder about 8 inches long. Wrap the sides of the foil tightly around the ice cream, taking care to make the cylinder as uniform as possible. Freeze at least 4 hours.

2. In a food processor or blender, chop chocolate cookies into coarse crumbs and spread them in a baking pan or dish at least 10 inches long. Remove the ice cream cylinder from the freezer, discard the foil, and roll the cylinder in the crumbs, gently pressing as you roll. Make the crumb coating as thick as possible.

3. Quickly place the ice cream roll on a chilled platter and return it to the freezer for at least 1 hour.

4. To serve, top the ice cream roll with chopped candies and cut it into 1-inch-thick slices. Pass the Chocolate-Peppermint Sauce separately, if desired.

Serves 8.

PIES

Frozen pies and tarts are wonderful to have on hand for unexpected guests and for dinner parties at which you would rather spend time with your guests than in the kitchen.

PEGGY'S WHITE CHOCOLATE TART

This wonderful dessert, created by Peggy Fallon, a noted cooking teacher, would be a hit at a bridal shower or summer luncheon.

> 2 ounces semisweet chocolate, melted
> Shaved white chocolate, for garnish
> Candied rose petals or violets, for garnish
> Fresh mint leaves, for garnish

Nut Crust

> 1 large egg
> 5 ounces (1 scant cup) almonds, finely chopped
> ½ cup unsalted butter, at room temperature
> 3 tablespoons sugar
> 1¼ cups flour
> ½ teaspoon almond extract
> ¼ teaspoon vanilla extract
> Pinch of salt
> Chopped zest of 1 orange, about 2 teaspoons (optional)

White Chocolate Mousse

> 9 ounces white chocolate, chopped very fine
> ¼ cup water
> 1½ cups whipping cream

Raspberry Purée

> 1 package (12 oz) frozen raspberries in syrup, thawed
> Superfine sugar, to taste
> Lemon juice or framboise, to taste

To assemble: Paint the inside of the Nut Crust with the melted chocolate. Pour in the White Chocolate Mousse and smooth it. Garnish the top of the tart with additional shaved white chocolate. Decorate with candied rose petals or violets and fresh mint leaves. Serve with Raspberry Purée.

Serves 8 to 10.

Nut Crust

1. Preheat oven to 350° F. Lightly coat a 10½- or 11-inch tart pan with nonstick vegetable cooking spray.

2. Beat egg; divide in half and reserve half for another use. In a food processor or blender, combine half of egg and remaining ingredients. When well mixed, press evenly into tart pan. Chill at least 30 minutes in the refrigerator or 15 minutes in the freezer.

3. Bake in the lower third of the oven until the edges of the crust pull away from the sides of the pan (20 to 25 minutes). Transfer pan to a rack and cool.

White Chocolate Mousse

1. Heat chocolate and the water in a glass or porcelain bowl over boiled, not boiling, water until chocolate just melts. Remove from heat and cool to room temperature.

2. Whip the cream to soft peaks. Combine one third of the cream with the melted chocolate, then fold in remaining whipped cream. Pour into a bowl and chill at least 3 hours.

Raspberry Purée Strain berries and their syrup through a sieve to remove the seeds. Push through as much of the fruit as possible. Add sugar and lemon juice to taste.

Makes about 1 cup.

MUD PIE

This is a favorite among coffee and chocolate lovers.

> 1 recipe Hot Fudge Sauce (see page 42)
> 1 quart Coffee Ice Cream (see page 22)
> ¾ cup whipping cream
> 1 teaspoon vanilla extract
> 1 tablespoon confectioners' sugar
> ⅓ cup toasted almonds, for decorating

Chocolate Cookie Crust

> 1 package (8½ oz) chocolate wafers
> 6 tablespoons unsalted butter, melted
> Pinch ground cinnamon

1. Pour a thin layer of Hot Fudge Sauce into the cooled Chocolate Cookie Crust and freeze until firm.

2. Spoon ice cream into the frozen crust and level the top. Press plastic wrap over ice cream and freeze at least 1½ hours.

3. Spread a generous layer of fudge sauce over ice cream. Freeze at least 30 minutes. Meanwhile, whip the cream with vanilla and sugar. Spread over the frozen pie. Decorate with almonds and freeze another 2 hours or longer.

Serves 8 to 10.

Chocolate Cookie Crust Preheat oven to 350° F. Butter the bottom, but not the sides, of a 9-inch pie plate. In a food processor or blender, crush chocolate wafers. In a medium bowl combine crushed wafers, melted butter, and cinnamon. Press crumb mixture evenly into pie plate. (Pressing another pie plate directly onto the crumbs for 1 to 2 minutes helps pack them.) Bake 8 to 10 minutes on center oven rack. Cool to room temperature.

Even dark chocolate devotees will be delighted by this white chocolate tart. What a beautiful way to end a meal.

The sky's the limit on enjoyment when your menu includes this Mile-High Strawberry Pie. This time-honored treat is a snap to make.

ICEBOX CHOCOLATE PIE

This pie can be completely made and decorated ahead of time.

> 2 cups (about 60) crushed vanilla wafers
> ⅓ cup unsalted butter, at room temperature
> 12 ounces semisweet chocolate
> 3 large eggs
> 2 teaspoons vanilla extract
> 2 cups whipping cream
> Grated semisweet chocolate, for garnish

1. Combine crushed wafers and butter. Press into an 8-inch springform pan or deep-dish pie pan.

2. In the top of a double boiler, melt chocolate over simmering water. Separate 2 of the eggs (reserve egg whites for step 3). In a small bowl beat the 2 yolks plus 1 whole egg, mixing well. Add to melted chocolate, then add vanilla.

3. In a separate bowl whip 1 cup of the cream. In another small bowl whisk the 2 reserved egg whites until stiff but not dry. Fold whipped cream into chocolate mixture, then fold in beaten egg whites. Pour into prepared crust and freeze at least 2 hours.

4. To serve, whip remaining cream to soft peaks. Top frozen pie with whipped cream (it may be piped on with a pastry bag for a more decorative effect) and sprinkle with grated chocolate.

Serves 8.

114

MILE-HIGH STRAWBERRY PIE

Any berry can be substituted in this quick dessert.

- 1 package (10 oz) frozen strawberries or raspberries in syrup, thawed
  About ½ cup sugar, or to taste
- 1 tablespoon lemon juice
- 2 large egg whites
- ¾ cup whipping cream
- 1 pie shell or graham cracker crust (9 in.), baked

In a large bowl combine berries, sugar, lemon juice, and egg whites. Beat with an electric mixer until soft peaks form and mixture is very thick (15 to 20 minutes). In a separate bowl whip the cream to soft peaks and fold into berry mixture. Gently pile filling high in pie crust and freeze until firm. About 30 minutes before serving, transfer pie from freezer to refrigerator.

Serves 8 to 10.

JAMAICAN COFFEE CREAM PIE

If you don't have time to make the crust, make just the cream filling and spoon it into dessert dishes for freezing.

- 1 recipe Chocolate Cookie Crust (see page 112)
- 8 large egg yolks, at room temperature
- ¼ cup sugar
- ¼ cup water
- ½ cup coffee-flavored liqueur
- 1 cup whipping cream
- ½ cup semisweet chocolate chips

1. Press Chocolate Cookie Crust into a 9-inch springform pan or deep-dish glass pie plate. Freeze.

2. Beat egg yolks in the large bowl of an electric mixer until light colored and tripled in volume (7 to 10 minutes). Meanwhile, in a small saucepan bring sugar and the water to a boil and let boil about 5 minutes.

3. With the electric mixer running, pour the hot sugar syrup into the beaten egg yolks in a thin, steady stream. Continue to beat until cold. Stir in liqueur and set aside.

4. Whip the cream to soft peaks. Gently fold one third of the whipped cream into yolk mixture to lighten it, then fold in the remaining whipped cream and chocolate chips.

5. Remove crust from freezer and spoon mixture into it. Tap pan gently against a cutting board to prevent air pockets from forming. Cover well and freeze at least 6 hours.

Serves 8 to 10.

CHOCOLATE-RUM PIE WITH PECAN CRUST

The nuts make this an especially delicious crust that can be used with many different fillings.

- 8 ounces semisweet chocolate, chopped
- 2 teaspoons instant coffee powder
- 1 teaspoon vanilla extract
- 2 tablespoons dark rum
- 4 large eggs
- 1½ cups whipping cream

Pecan Crust

- 2½ cups finely chopped pecans
- ½ cup unsalted butter, softened
- 2 tablespoons dark rum
- ⅓ cup firmly packed dark brown sugar

1. In the top of a double boiler set over simmering water, melt chocolate; cool completely. In a small bowl combine coffee, vanilla, and rum, stirring until coffee is dissolved; add to melted chocolate.

2. In a medium bowl beat eggs until well blended, then combine with chocolate mixture. Mix well. In another bowl beat cream to soft peaks and fold it into chocolate mixture. Pour filling into Pecan Crust. Freeze, covered, at least 4 hours.

3. To serve, let pie stand at room temperature about 15 minutes or until it is soft enough to slice.

Serves 10.

Pecan Crust In a medium bowl combine pecans, butter, rum, and brown sugar. Press mixture into the bottom and up the sides of a 10-inch glass pie plate. Freeze until needed.

ELEGANT ENDINGS

The following recipes take a little additional time to prepare, but the results are well worth the effort.

CHERRIES JUBILEE

This provides a colorful, dramatic ending to any dinner party.

- 2 tablespoons sugar
- 2 tablespoons kirsch
- 1 tablespoon cornstarch
- 1 can (16 oz) of pitted sweet or sour red cherries and their juice
- 1 pint French Vanilla Ice Cream (see page 22)
- ½ cup brandy

1. In a small saucepan over moderate heat, warm sugar, kirsch, cornstarch, and cherries with their juice until hot but not boiling. Put in a bowl and bring to the table.

2. Scoop ice cream into dessert dishes. Warm a ladleful of brandy over a medium burner or candle. Light a match, ignite the brandy, and pour it over the cherry sauce. Stir until the flame dies down. Spoon over ice cream and serve at once.

Serves 4 to 6.

POIRES BELLE HÉLÈNE

This dessert combines pears with ice cream and chocolate sauce.

- 2 cups sugar
- 3 cups water
- 4 ripe pears, peeled, halved, and cored
- 1 tablespoon vanilla extract
- 1 quart French Vanilla Ice Cream (see page 22)
- 1 recipe Old-Fashioned Chocolate Sauce (see page 30)

1. In a medium saucepan bring sugar and the water to a boil. Add pear halves. Cover and simmer for 15 to 20 minutes. Remove from heat and let cool. Add vanilla. Chill.

2. For a serving, cover a scoop of ice cream with a pear half. Drizzle with Old-Fashioned Chocolate Sauce.

Serves 8.

This Italian Bombe takes a bit of time, but it's well worth the effort. Its zabaglione, pear, and chocolate layers make it a truly memorable dessert.

ITALIAN BOMBE

This recipe comes from Gloria Bowers, a food consultant who is well known for her desserts. The very impressive—and delicious—bombe contains two ice cream layers (chocolate and zabaglione) and a layer of pear sorbet. The Zabaglione Ice Cream is actually two classic French creams: crème anglaise and crème patissière, combined and frozen into ice cream. The vanilla sugar for Zabaglione Ice Cream should be made a week ahead. If desired, garnish the finished bombe with whipped cream and chocolate shavings.

Three-Egg Chocolate Ice Cream

  ½ cup half-and-half
  1 ounce bittersweet chocolate, chopped
  3 large egg yolks
  3 tablespoons sugar
  ¾ cup whipping cream
  2 tablespoons unsalted butter
  ¼ teaspoon vanilla extract

Pear Sorbet

  ⅓ cup sugar
  ⅓ cup water
  2 tablespoons lemon juice
  1 tablespoon pear-flavored liqueur
  1 teaspoon grated lemon zest
  3 poached fresh pears or 1 can (29 oz) pear halves, drained, puréed, and chilled

Zabaglione Ice Cream

  3 vanilla beans
  2 cups plus 1 tablespoon sugar
  ¾ cup milk
  ½ cup whipping cream
  3 large egg yolks
  1½ teaspoons flour
  ⅓ cup whipping cream
  ½ teaspoon vanilla extract
  ⅓ cup Marsala wine

1. Chill a 1½-quart bombe mold in the freezer for several hours or overnight. Brush the inside of the mold with vegetable oil and line it with two 1-inch-wide strips of aluminum foil or waxed paper crisscrossed and extending 3 inches above the rim of the mold at both ends.

2. Press three quarters of the Three-Egg Chocolate Ice Cream into the mold, evenly covering the sides and bottom. Freeze until firm.

3. Press the Zabaglione Ice Cream into an even layer over the Three-Egg Chocolate Ice Cream. Freeze until very firm.

4. Fill in the center of the bombe with the Pear Sorbet. Freeze until very firm.

5. Cover the top surface with the remaining Three-Egg Chocolate Ice Cream. Cover with plastic wrap and freeze overnight or until ice cream is very firm.

6. To unmold, invert the frozen bombe onto a serving plate. Cover the mold with a hot towel. To help loosen the bombe, pull gently on the aluminum foil strips. Decorate the bombe with whipped cream and chocolate shavings, if desired.

Serves 10 to 12.

Three-Egg Chocolate Ice Cream

1. In a small saucepan heat half-and-half and chocolate until chocolate is melted, then bring to a quick boil. Remove from heat and cool. Chill at least 3 to 4 hours or overnight.

2. In a medium bowl beat egg yolks and sugar until a stiff ribbon forms on the surface when the beater is lifted. In a 1-quart saucepan bring cream to a boil. Whisk cream into egg-yolk mixture, then return mixture to saucepan and cook over medium heat, stirring constantly, just until mixture coats the back of a wooden spoon. Do not boil. Remove from heat and stir in butter and vanilla.

3. Transfer to an ice cream machine and freeze according to manufacturer's instructions. Let stand 2 hours in freezer to "ripen" before using.

Makes 1 pint.

Pear Sorbet In a small saucepan heat sugar and the water until sugar melts. Remove from heat and cool. Add lemon juice, liqueur, and lemon zest. Chill. Stir sugar syrup into chilled purée. Transfer to an ice cream machine and freeze according to manufacturer's instructions. Let sorbet "ripen" in freezer for several hours.

Makes about 1 pint.

Zabaglione Ice Cream

1. A week before you plan to make the ice cream, bury 2 of the vanilla beans in 2 cups of the sugar in an airtight container. Set aside.

2. To make crème anglaise: Split remaining vanilla bean lengthwise. In a medium saucepan combine ½ cup of the milk, the ½ cup cream, and vanilla bean and bring to a boil. Reduce heat and simmer 5 minutes. Remove vanilla bean and, if you want a stronger vanilla flavor, scrape some of its seeds back into the pan.

3. Beat together 2 of the egg yolks and 3 tablespoons of the prepared vanilla sugar until smooth and thick. (Reserve remaining vanilla sugar for other uses.) Whisk in the hot milk mixture, then return mixture to the saucepan and stir over medium heat until mixture coats the back of a spoon. Transfer to a bowl, and cool over ice water until cold. Chill until ready to use.

4. To make crème patissière: In a medium saucepan bring remaining milk to a boil. In a bowl combine remaining egg yolk, 1 tablespoon of the sugar, and flour and beat until smooth. Whisk hot milk into yolk mixture, then return mixture to the saucepan and cook over medium heat until very thick. Remove from heat, cool, then chill thoroughly. In a separate bowl whip the ⅓ cup cream. Whisk vanilla and Marsala wine into mixture, then fold in whipped cream.

5. Fold crème patissière into crème anglaise. Transfer to an ice cream machine and freeze according to manufacturer's instructions. Let ice cream "ripen" in freezer for several hours.

Makes 1½ quarts.

DOME PÉRIGNON

This dessert is more than a play on words—it is a stunning finale for a special meal. For this recipe it is perfectly acceptable to use one of the sweeter Champagnes, such as sec or extra dry.

- 1 Vanilla Sponge Cake (see page 101)
- 1 recipe Raspberry Purée (see page 112)

Pineapple Champagne Sherbet

- 2 cups chilled Champagne
- ½ cup chilled Simple Sugar Syrup (see page 15)
- ¼ cup lemon juice
- 2½ cups finely chopped fresh pineapple with its own juice or 1 can (15¼ oz) crushed pineapple and its unsweetened juice, well chilled
- 1 cup whole milk, well chilled
  Pinch of salt

1. Soften Pineapple Champagne Sherbet in the refrigerator for 15 minutes or in a microwave oven for 15 seconds. Place unrolled cake on a large sheet of heavy-duty aluminum foil. Spread cake with 2 cups of the softened sherbet (reserve remainder for step 2). Reroll cake, cover tightly with foil, and freeze at least 2 hours. At the same time freeze an empty 2-quart bowl.

2. Remove the chilled bowl from the freezer and line it with 1 large sheet of plastic wrap. Remove the foil from frozen cake roll. Cut roll into ½-inch-thick slices. Beginning at the bottom, line the bowl with the cake slices, fitting them closely together. Fill the center with the remaining sherbet. Cover tightly and freeze at least 6 hours.

3. To serve, invert the bowl on a chilled plate. Lift off the bowl and carefully peel off the plastic wrap. Cut the dome into wedges and serve with Raspberry Purée.

Serves 12.

Pineapple Champagne Sherbet

Combine all ingredients. Transfer to an ice cream machine and freeze according to manufacturer's instructions. (If your ice cream machine has only a 1-quart capacity, make this in two batches.)

Makes about 2 quarts.

WHAT-A BOMBE

The smooth, soothing flavors of this dessert complement a cup of good coffee or a glass of Cognac.

- 1 quart French Vanilla Ice Cream (see page 22)
- 1 quart Coffee Ice Cream (see page 22)
- 1 quart Mocha Ice Cream (see page 40)
- ½ cup slivered almonds, toasted
- 2 recipes Chocolate-Rum Sauce (see page 28)

1. Brush a 3-quart bombe mold or metal bowl with vegetable oil and chill in the freezer at least 1 hour.

2. Defrost French Vanilla Ice Cream in the refrigerator about 15 minutes, until soft but not melted. Working quickly with a spatula, line the frozen mold evenly with the softened ice cream. Immediately return to the freezer. Soften the Coffee Ice Cream the same way and evenly cover the French Vanilla Ice Cream with it. Immediately return the mold to the freezer. Soften the Mocha Ice Cream and fill the center of the mold with it. Cover with plastic wrap and freeze at least 4 hours.

3. Unmold ice cream onto a chilled platter. Sprinkle the top of the bombe with toasted almonds. Return to the freezer until ready to serve.

4. To serve, dip a knife in hot water, blot it dry, and slice the bombe. Warm and dry the knife before each slice. Serve slices of bombe on chilled dessert plates; pass Chocolate-Rum Sauce separately.

Serves 12 to 14.

DOUBLE-CHOCOLATE CRÊPES WITH ORANGE CONFIT

Serve this very sophisticated dessert to very special friends.

- 1 quart Dark Chocolate Ice Cream (see page 39)
- 2 cups Hot Fudge Sauce (see page 42), for topping (optional)
- 1 cup whipped cream, for topping (optional)
  Cocoa powder, for dusting (optional)

Chocolate Crêpes

- ½ cup cold water
- ½ cup milk
- 2 large eggs
- 1 teaspoon vanilla extract
- ¼ teaspoon salt
- 1 cup flour
- 1 ounce semisweet chocolate, finely chopped
- 4 tablespoons unsalted butter, softened

Orange Confit

- 6 large oranges
- 2½ cups freshly squeezed orange juice
- 1¼ cups sugar
- ⅓ cup grenadine

To assemble: Defrost 16 Chocolate Crêpes, if frozen. Roll each crêpe around 1 scoop of ice cream. Place 2 crêpes, seam side down, on each dessert plate. Spoon 1 to 2 tablespoons Orange Confit to the side of each crêpe. Top each with about ¼ cup Hot Fudge Sauce or a whipped cream rosette lightly dusted with cocoa powder (if desired).

Serves 8.

Chocolate Crêpes

1. In a food processor or blender, mix the water, milk, eggs, vanilla, and salt. Add flour and mix well. Place mixture in a bowl; cover. Set aside in a cool spot at least 4 hours or refrigerate overnight. (Bring to room temperature before proceeding.)

2. In the top of a double boiler or in a pan set over barely simmering water, melt chocolate and butter together. Cool to room temperature.

3. In a bowl thoroughly blend chocolate mixture with egg mixture.

4. Heat a seasoned crêpe pan or a lightly buttered frying pan over medium-high heat. Pour in a small ladleful (about 1½ ounces) of chocolate-egg batter. Quickly roll and turn the pan to spread the batter. Pour excess batter back into bowl. Cook each crêpe until dark brown specks appear on top, then turn crêpe over briefly to cook the other side. Cool.

Makes 16 to 24 crêpes.

<u>Note</u> Crêpes can be made in advance and kept in the freezer for months. Stack crêpes with a piece of waxed paper or plastic wrap between each two so they will not stick together.

Orange Confit

1. Remove zest from oranges; finely chop and reserve zest. Remove and discard white pith; divide oranges into segments, removing and discarding seeds.

2. Heat orange juice and sugar in a medium saucepan over low heat, brushing down sides of pan with a pastry brush dipped in cold water, until sugar melts. Increase heat to medium-high and boil mixture until it reaches the thread stage (230° F on a candy thermometer). Remove from heat. Add orange segments, reserved zest, and grenadine. Let cool, then refrigerate until needed. Serve at room temperature.

Makes 2 cups.

Double-Chocolate Crêpes are an irresistible treat for chocoholics. The slightly tart orange confit is a perfect foil for the rich Dark Chocolate Ice Cream hidden inside.

119

RUM MOUSSE L'ORANGE WITH RUM BALLS

Rum lovers will find this combination irresistible.

 ¾ cup sugar
 ½ cup water
 6 large egg yolks
 ½ cup dark rum
 1 tablespoon orange-flavored liqueur or freshly squeezed orange juice
   Zest of 1 orange
 2 cups chilled whipping cream

Rum Balls

 2½ cups (about 75) finely crushed vanilla wafers
 2 tablespoons unsweetened cocoa powder
 1 cup confectioners' sugar
 1 cup finely chopped walnuts or pecans
 3 tablespoons light corn syrup
 ¼ cup dark rum
   Confectioners' sugar, for coating

1. Combine sugar and the water in a medium saucepan; boil until sugar dissolves, then boil 5 minutes longer. Set aside to cool about 15 minutes.

2. In the top of a double boiler or a pan placed over simmering water, combine sugar syrup, egg yolks, and rum. Cook, stirring constantly, until mixture coats the back of a spoon. Remove from heat, set the bowl over ice, and beat until mixture has cooled. Mix in liqueur and orange zest. In a separate bowl whip the cream. Fold orange-syrup mixture into whipped cream.

3. Freeze in a 1-quart serving bowl or individual dessert cups. Garnish each serving with 2 or 3 Rum Balls.

Serves 8.

Rum Balls In a large bowl mix together crushed wafers, cocoa, the 1 cup confectioners' sugar, and nuts. Add corn syrup, then add rum. Mix well. Form into 1-inch balls and roll in confectioners' sugar to coat. Store in an airtight container or freeze and bring to room temperature before serving.

Makes 42 to 48 balls.

FROZEN BLACK-AND-WHITE MARBLE MOUSSE

Chocolate and vanilla—the best of both worlds is captured in this sensational dessert.

 9 ounces semisweet chocolate, finely chopped
 10 large egg yolks
 ¾ cup sugar
 1 tablespoon vanilla extract
 2 cups whipping cream, chilled
 ¾ cup miniature chocolate chips
 2 cups Hot Fudge Sauce (see page 42), for topping (optional)

1. Place a 6-cup ring mold or 9-inch springform pan in the freezer to chill.

2. In the top of a double boiler or a pan set over barely simmering water, melt semisweet chocolate and stir until smooth. Set aside to cool.

3. In a large bowl beat yolks with an electric mixer until combined. With the mixer running, add sugar in a slow, steady stream. Continue to beat until a ribbon forms on surface when beater is raised. Mix in vanilla extract. Divide mixture in half. Fold one half into the melted chocolate.

4. Whip the cream to soft peaks. Divide in half. Fold half into chocolate mixture and other half into vanilla mixture. Fold chocolate chips into vanilla mixture.

5. Using a large spoon or rubber spatula, drop mounds of chocolate mixture into the chilled mold and add mounds of vanilla–chocolate chip mixture. Tap mold against a cutting board several times to eliminate any air pockets.

6. Swirl a skewer or a thin knife through mousse to create a marbled effect. Cover well with plastic wrap and freeze at least 6 hours.

7. With a knife loosen mousse from the sides of the mold. Quickly dip the mold in warm tap water and invert it onto a chilled serving platter. If frozen solid let mousse soften in the refrigerator about 15 minutes before unmolding. Slice and serve. Top with Hot Fudge Sauce (if desired).

Serves 10.

BANANAS FOSTER

This adult sundae is a traditional New Orleans dessert, first served at the Commander's Palace restaurant.

 ⅓ cup unsalted butter
 ⅓ cup freshly squeezed orange juice
 2 tablespoons lemon juice
 ¾ cup firmly packed brown sugar
 ⅓ cup banana-flavored liqueur
 ⅓ cup brandy
 6 bananas, peeled and cut diagonally into 2-inch-thick slices
 1 quart French Vanilla Ice Cream (see page 22)

1. In a large skillet over medium heat, melt butter. When foam subsides stir in orange juice, lemon juice, and brown sugar. Simmer until mixture bubbles and coats a metal spoon (about 3 minutes).

2. Add liqueur and ignite carefully. When flames subside add brandy and ignite again. When flames go out add bananas and toss to coat.

3. To serve, scoop ice cream into dessert bowls. Spoon sauce and coated bananas over ice cream and serve immediately.

Serves 8.

This marbled black-and-white mousse interweaves the rich flavors of chocolate and vanilla. Try it topped with Hot Fudge Sauce.

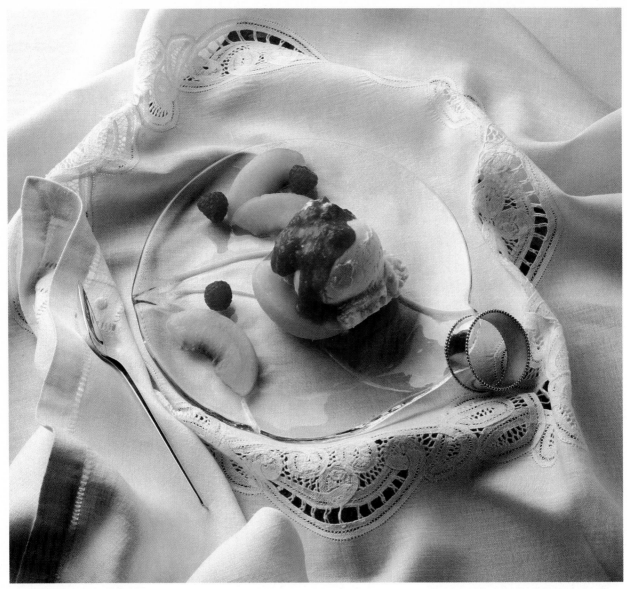

Sweet and tart, rich and fresh—no wonder Peach Melba is a timeless classic dessert.

DRIED-FRUIT MOUSSE

Dried apricots make this dessert particularly delicious. Other dried fruits will work well too; try substituting your favorite or a mixture.

> 1 pound dried apricots
> ¾ cup sugar
> ¼ cup lemon juice or white wine
> 1 tablespoon apricot-flavored brandy or other liqueur
> 5 large egg whites, at room temperature
> 2 cups whipping cream, chilled Bourbon Pecan Sauce (see page 39), for topping (optional)

1. Place apricots in a 2-quart saucepan, cover with tap water, and simmer for 30 minutes.

2. Drain apricots and place them in the bowl of a food processor or blender with sugar, lemon juice, and brandy. Purée until smooth, then pour into a large mixing bowl.

3. In a separate bowl beat egg whites to soft peaks. Fold one third of the beaten whites into purée to lighten it, then fold in remaining whites.

4. In a separate bowl whip the cream to stiff peaks. Fold one third of the whipped cream into purée mixture to lighten it, then fold in remaining whipped cream.

5. Spoon mousse into a 2-quart freezerproof serving bowl. Freeze until firm (about 4 hours). Serve in chilled dessert dishes topped with Bourbon Pecan Sauce (if desired).

Serves 8 to 10.

CHOCOLATE-PECAN PÂTE

This frozen dessert should be thawed about 8 hours in the refrigerator before serving. It's well worth the wait.

> 1 cup pecan halves, lightly toasted (see Rocky Road Ice Cream, Note, page 22)
> 12 ounces semisweet chocolate, finely chopped
> ¾ cup whipping cream
> 4 tablespoons unsalted butter, cut into 4 to 6 pieces
> ⅓ cup sugar
> ¼ cup dark rum
> 4 large eggs, separated, at room temperature
> Pinch of salt
> 1 recipe Chocolate-Rum Sauce (see page 28) or
> 1 recipe Vanilla Sauce (see page 30), for topping (optional)
> 1 recipe Raspberry Purée (see page 112), for topping (optional)
> 1 cup whipping cream, for topping (optional)

1. Butter a 1- or 1½-quart glass loaf pan and line the bottom with buttered parchment paper. Arrange pecans in rows face down on the parchment.

2. Place chocolate, the ¾ cup cream, and butter in a large heatproof bowl. Set on top of a 2-quart saucepan containing 2 inches of barely simmering water. Stir occasionally until chocolate melts, then beat until mixture is well blended. (A double boiler can be used for this, but the mixing bowl gives more room to beat the mixture.)

3. Remove from heat and beat in sugar. Add rum. Add egg yolks one at a time, beating well after each addition. Set aside.

4. In another bowl beat egg whites and salt to soft peaks. Fold one third of the whites into the chocolate mixture to lighten it, then fold in remaining whites. Gently spoon into prepared loaf pan, taking care not to disturb pecans. Cover with plastic wrap and freeze.

5. To serve, defrost in the refrigerator for 8 hours. Unmold onto a chilled plate. With a hot knife, cut pâte into ⅓-inch-thick slices. Serve with sauce, Raspberry Purée, and whipped cream (if desired).

Serves 8 to 10.

FROZEN CHOCOLATE CHARLOTTE

This stunning dessert is sure to please any chocolate lover.

> ½ cups plus 1 tablespoon granulated sugar
> 1 package (5 oz) ladyfingers
> ¼ cup dark rum or orange-flavored liqueur (optional)
> 6 ounces semisweet chocolate, coarsely chopped
> ⅔ cup strong coffee
> 4 large egg yolks
> 2 cups whipping cream
> ¼ cup thinly sliced almonds, toasted (optional)
> Confectioners' sugar, for dusting (optional)
> Whipped cream

1. Lightly oil a charlotte, soufflé, or other 1½-quart straight-sided mold. Coat the sides but not the bottom with 1 tablespoon of the granulated sugar.

2. Lightly brush ladyfingers with rum, if used. Arrange in a single layer standing upright against the sides of the mold. Chill in the freezer while making the filling.

3. In a small, heavy-bottomed saucepan, melt chocolate with ⅓ cup of the coffee, stirring until smooth. Set aside.

4. In another small saucepan combine remaining granulated sugar with remaining coffee and boil until mixture reaches soft-ball stage (238° F on a candy thermometer). Meanwhile, using an electric mixer, beat egg yolks until they are thick and pale yellow. Gradually add hot sugar

syrup in a thin, steady stream, beating constantly. Add melted chocolate mixture and continue to beat until mixture is cool.

5. In a separate bowl whip the cream. Fold one third of the whipped cream into the chocolate mixture to lighten it, then fold in the remaining whipped cream. Pour into prepared mold, cover tightly with plastic wrap, and freeze at least 4 hours.

6. To serve, remove the plastic wrap from mold and run a thin, sharp knife between ladyfingers and mold. (If this does not free charlotte, quickly dip mold in warm water.) Invert onto a chilled plate, remove mold, and garnish top of charlotte with toasted almonds and a sprinkling of confectioners' sugar (if desired). Slice and serve. Garnish each serving with a spoonful of whipped cream (if desired).

Serves 8.

PEACH MELBA

The great French chef Escoffier created this dessert in honor of a popular opera singer, Nellie Melba.

> 3 cups water
> 2 cups sugar
> 4 large peaches, peeled, halved, and pitted
> 1 tablespoon vanilla extract
> 1 cup fresh raspberries
> 1 quart French Vanilla Ice Cream (see page 22)

1. In a medium saucepan combine the water and sugar; bring to a boil. Add peach halves. Lower the heat and simmer, covered, for 10 to 15 minutes. Remove from heat; let cool. Stir in vanilla, then chill.

2. In a small saucepan heat raspberries to boiling, stirring constantly and mashing berries with a spoon. Let cool and then chill.

3. To serve, place prepared peach halves on chilled dessert plates. Top each half with a scoop of ice cream. Drizzle raspberry topping all over each serving.

Serves 8.

INDEX

127

U.S. MEASURE AND METRIC MEASURE CONVERSION CHART

	Formulas for Exact Measures				Rounded Measures for Quick Reference		
	Symbol	**When you know:**	**Multiply by:**	**To find:**			
Mass (Weight)	oz	ounces	28.35	grams	1 oz		= 30 g
	lb	pounds	0.45	kilograms	4 oz		= 115 g
	g	grams	0.035	ounces	8 oz		= 225 g
	kg	kilograms	2.2	pounds	16 oz	= 1 lb	= 450 g
					32 oz	= 2 lb	= 900 g
					36 oz	= $2\frac{1}{4}$ lb	= 1,000g (1 kg)
Volume	tsp	teaspoons	5.0	milliliters	$\frac{1}{4}$ tsp	= $\frac{1}{24}$ oz	= 1 ml
	tbsp	tablespoons	15.0	milliliters	$\frac{1}{2}$ tsp	= $\frac{1}{12}$ oz	= 2 ml
	fl oz	fluid ounces	29.57	milliliters	1 tsp	= $\frac{1}{6}$ oz	= 5 ml
	c	cups	0.24	liters	1 tbsp	= $\frac{1}{2}$ oz	= 15 ml
	pt	pints	0.47	liters	1 c	= 8 oz	= 250 ml
	qt	quarts	0.95	liters	2 c (1 pt)	= 16 oz	= 500 ml
	gal	gallons	3.785	liters	4 c (1 qt)	= 32 oz	= 1 liter
	ml	milliliters	0.034	fluid ounces	4 qt (1 gal)	= 128 oz	= $3\frac{3}{4}$ liter
Length	in.	inches	2.54	centimeters	$\frac{3}{8}$ in.	= 1 cm	
	ft	feet	30.48	centimeters	1 in.	= 2.5 cm	
	yd	yards	0.9144	meters	2 in.	= 5 cm	
	mi	miles	1.609	kilometers	$2\frac{1}{2}$ in.	= 6.5 cm	
	km	kilometers	0.621	miles	12 in. (1 ft)	= 30 cm	
	m	meters	1.094	yards	1 yd	= 90 cm	
	cm	centimeters	0.39	inches	100 ft	= 30 m	
					1 mi	= 1.6 km	
Temperature	°F	Fahrenheit	$\frac{5}{9}$ (after subtracting 32)	Celsius	32°F	= 0°C	
					68°F	= 20°C	
	°C	Celsius	$\frac{9}{5}$ (then add 32)	Fahrenheit	212°F	= 100°C	
Area	$in.^2$	square inches	6.452	square centimeters	1 $in.^2$	= 6.5 cm^2	
	ft^2	square feet	929.0	square centimeters	1 ft^2	= 930 cm^2	
	yd^2	square yards	8361.0	square centimeters	1 yd^2	= 8360 cm^2	
	a.	acres	0.4047	hectares	1 a.	= 4050 m^2	